P9-BZC-302

DIGGING
TO CHINA

ALSO BY J.D. BROWN

Henry Miller

*Rip, Strip, and Row: A Builder's Guide
to the Cosine Wherry*

Anthology of Eugene Writers

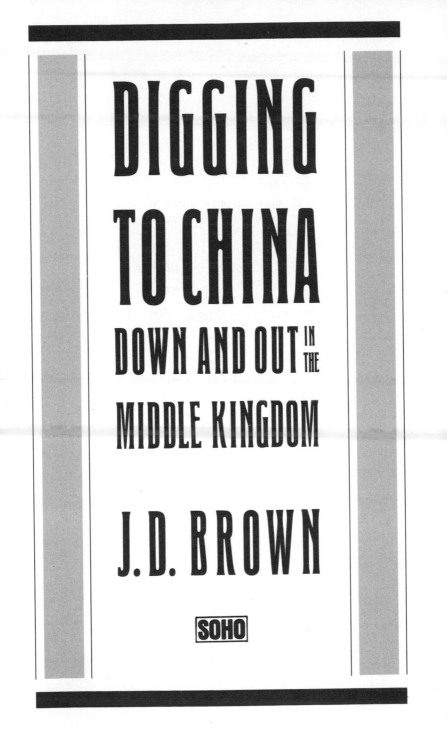

DIGGING TO CHINA

DOWN AND OUT IN THE MIDDLE KINGDOM

J. D. BROWN

SOHO

Portions of this work in earlier versions have appeared in *The Boston Globe, The Christian Science Monitor, Emmy Magazine, Iowa Review, Newsday, Northwest Review, The Salt Lake Tribune, Seattle Weekly, and Western Humanities Review.*

Copyright © 1984, 1985, 1987, 1988,
1989, 1990 and 1991 by J.D. Brown
All rights reserved.

Published by
Soho Press, Inc.
853 Broadway
New York, NY 10003

Library of Congress Cataloging-in-Publication Data

Brown, J.D. (James Dale), 1948–
Digging to China : down and out in the middle kingdom / J.D.
Brown.
p.   cm.
ISBN 0–939149–51–6 :
1. China—Description and travel—1976–   2. Brown, J.D. (James
Dale), 1948–   —Journeys–China.
DS712.B78   1991
915.'04'5—dc20
                                                    91–7805
                                                    CIP

Manufactured in the United States
10 9 8 7 6 5 4 3 2 1

Book design and composition by
The Sarabande Press

To Mike and Ellen and to Ken, integral parts of a gang of four; to Bob and Gladys, for their irreligious offerings; and most of all to Margaret.

— : : —

But its odd—the relief at losing possessions. I shd like to start life, in peace, almost bare—free to go anywhere.

—Virginia Woolf, Diary

In the interior of that country is a very great city, but it is not easy to reach, and few and far between are those who return from it.

—Pliny of Rome

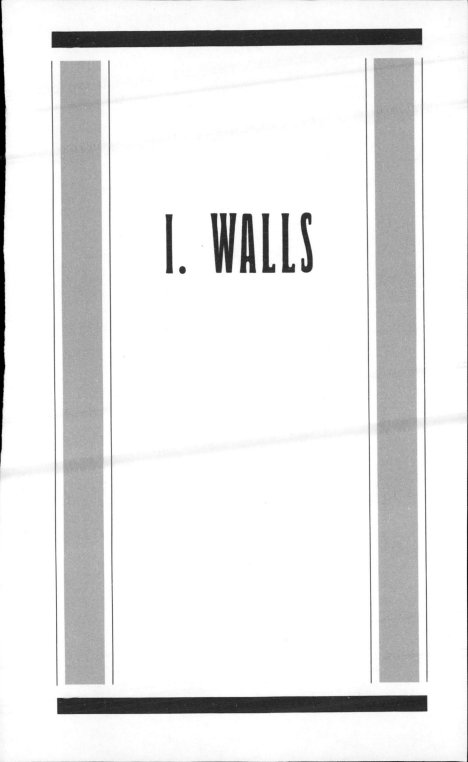

I. WALLS

ROCKY IN CANTON

I land in China not speaking a word of Chinese, and I am promptly stranded in Canton. My connecting flight has been cancelled and not rescheduled. My employers at the Medical College in Xi'an, the ancient capital in the interior of the People's Republic, expect me to arrive today. I am to replace some poor soul who lasted scarcely seven days. I don't know when or even how I will reach the interior.

The information desk shut down for the day the minute I arrived. This is how everything begins and ends here: abruptly, shatteringly. Alone, stricken, I take to heart two lines from a seventh century poet, Du Shen-yen: "Only to the wanderer comes/Ever new this shock of beauty."

I am condemned to pace the Canton air terminal, a faultless copy of an American bus depot circa 1956, with cigarette butts artfully ground into its marble floors. I have no notion of how to proceed. In the parking lot, air-conditioned

3

buses whiz in and out, gulping down whole tour groups, until I am the only foreigner left.

At twilight the curtains of smog part on the horizon. I spot a billboard plastered with the image of a tall building and hail a dented '64 Dodge taxi. The driver speaks no English. I point to the big advertisement in the distance, close my eyes, and in this way, I am finally delivered to the China Hotel, as if by a miraculous wind.

Inside, every detail is deluxe, from the underground parking garage to the nineteen-floor office tower awaiting the arrival of representatives from foreign oil companies. There is a bowling alley in the basement, a sauna on the second floor. A German chef presides over fourteen dining halls. Two hundred thirteen uniformed bellhops in white gloves do the postrevolutionary donkey work, and an English-language newspaper appears under my door in the predawn.

At dawn I cross the red granite lobby, under a high crystal chandelier, and enter an office marked Travel Arrangements — my first stop of the new day. A dozen idle experts immediately come to my aid. I hand over my ticket, my passport, my letter from the President of the Xi'an Medical College. When will my flight depart?

Repeatedly they telephone the airline, often in groups, two mouths per phone; not once does anyone connect. I stand with my hands behind my back, my thumbs dug into a belt loop. The chief agent draws me aside, whispers an obscure strategem, and I nod . . . which is how I end up cruising the back avenues of Canton in a Mercedes-Benz taxi, courtesy of the New China Hotel, destination: the moon.

We pull up at a two-story edifice. I'm let out on the curb. I go in by myself, not knowing what else to do. Two women are sweeping trash across the floor of this lesser lobby, then back again. No one is on duty. From the immense airplane logo above an abacus of closed windows, however, I know I have entered the southern headquarters of CAAC, the world's worst airline, famed for early departures and arrivals in the wrong city. It's yin and yang, I suppose, but mostly yang. This is not the carrier for those suffering from deadlines and other delusions. The airports of China lack such frills as radar, and no CAAC pilot will fly when it's too dark, foggy, rainy, cloudy or otherwise yangy—or, for that matter, take off during lunch.

I climb to the second floor. A ticket window on the far wall snaps open, as though expecting me, but before I reach it, another stranded tourist streaks out of the shadows, leans in, and begins barking in Louder English (the sort some of us believe all foreigners secretly understand). Meanwhile, I tear a sheet from my notebook, write out my destination, and hand it through the window. It is returned with a new departure time: 9:15 the next morning.

My limousine awaits. (This is going to cost me a fortune, and I don't possess a single credit card.) In my cushy room at the un-China Hotel, a pirated version of *Rocky* is pounding from the closed-circuit TV screen, broadcast in Louder English as well—which even I can no longer understand. I'm not in the least certain I'll ever leave Canton.

As the sun rises a second time in Canton, I watch a troop of the People's Liberation Army perform a regimental shadow-box in the hotel parking lot. I dress and hit the streets. No one pays me much attention. It is like strolling through the ghettos of someone else's dream.

Canton is dingy but in a modern frenzy, every corner a construction site. With cranes, trucks, and labor teams, it's Houston on the Orient Express. The Big Characters strung in banners over the streets might as well read TIME IS MONEY AND GET RICH QUICK, COMRADE. Workers in wicker hardhats sift and mix cement, shovel out foundations, and climb bamboo stalks lashed together into scaffoldings.

I am at the airport by 7:00 A.M., check through my trunk, and join another line to confirm my ticket. I am told the Xi'an flight has been cancelled again until late that afternoon. I stop caring, although I lack enough money to spend another night in Canton.

Luckily, there is another American in the line for Xi'an. We commiserate. Roger, accompanied by two Chinese associates from Hong Kong, is a computer specialist scheduled to give a training session at a factory in Xi'an. We take a taxi downtown to see the open market. The main attractions this Monday are monkeys, eels, and handwrung snake-bile hot to the touch. We exit at the dog stalls, where whole specimens swing on hooks. We emerge on the most crowded street in China and end up beside the ghastly gray Pearl River. All the way, Roger the Scrutible shouts orders to his two cronies and curses CAAC, his blood pressure at a rolling boil.

In the afternoon we play cards at the airport. I can see our plane parked on the field. A soldier with a rifle stands motionless under one wing.

At sunset, our flight is officially cancelled for the day. I talk

Roger into splitting the cost of a room. I know he'll love the
odorless new China Hotel. At dinner, over fish eyes and frog
legs, Roger's associates fill us in on Xi'an. They are sorry to
hear I have agreed to live there: no food, nothing to see, no
night life—no day life either—worse than Canton, which
they regard as well beyond the border of the habitable world.

Rocky II, the immortal sequel, is playing tonight but
Roger isn't watching; he clatters like an overheated sub-
machine gun, cursing the largest bureaucracy and worst
airline in the universe. He is close to melting down into the
wall-to-wall carpeting, his complexion matching Rocky's:
an iridescent white.

A few minutes after Roger disappears down the hall to
harangue his Hong Kong lackeys, the door flies open and in
trots the hotel electrician. With a grin and a thumb, he
points to the pass card pinned to his suit. He is about seventeen years old. Armed with a screwdriver and pliers, he
attacks the master console between the beds. The room-
lights pinball on and off, *Rocky* fades in and out, and the
electrician starts talking to me in what sounds like reverse
English, asking me an important, thoroughly unintelligible
question. Now and then I nod. Glancing at the TV screen, he
strikes his open palm with a fist, and yells, "Rocky—Pow!"

"Right!" I answer.

"Rocky—Pow!"

You got it, kid. A real knockout.

Po-Wow!

Po-Wow!

Po-Wow!

Out in the hall, though it's nearly midnight, there are teenage girls in bellhop uniforms pushing carpet-sweepers over the runners. The sweepers look like props from "I Love Lucy."

Roger hasn't returned. I leave the TV running. Perhaps he'll have an answer to the electrician's big question, which I think I finally understood, to wit: Is it true that Americans eat steak standing up?

You betcha.

— : : —

The next day our plane departs Canton just two hours late. After a furious charge down an endless runway, the grinding propellers on each wing somehow lift us over a rice field, barely clearing a couple of water buffalos in harness. I've converted the last of my funds into foreign exchange certificates. After settling up with Roger, I'm broke.

Ours is an elderly Russian plane. Its seats are sprung, never to return to their full upright positions. From the aisle, they look like two rows of crooked teeth.

Midway to Xi'an, the pilot brings us down for lunch at Changsha, Mao's birthplace. The cafeteria is in an unheated outbuilding. We eat in one room, the regular Chinese in another, all served from the same kitchen. Changsha is so uniformly desolate on this chilly, overcast day that I nearly weep.

The plane engines obliterate thought. I actually doze off. When I awake, I think: Do with me what you will, China. . . . Now the plane is circling. Xi'an is under clouds. I can't locate it. Even when the clouds clear, we keep circling, but I'm no longer afraid. I'm calmer than I've ever been. I could die here. In fact, I'm certain that I will. I shed all apprehension in Canton, even the pointless concern over my own fate. I'm as empty as I've ever been, and I can't wait to see what happens next—something, nothing, it doesn't matter.

A LAND
WITHOUT
PIZZA

When we land in Xi'an, I am met by Professor Zhong of the English department at the Medical College. He's a gracious, round-faced soul, about sixty, dressed in a dark suit and tie, a man with a fine command of English who seems concerned about whether I like Chinese food.

Professor Zhong places me in the back seat of a sedan modeled after a 1950s Mercedes. The lace curtains are discreetly drawn on the rear and side windows. We drive past farms and into the forlorn suburbs; I feel like a sequestered dignitary. I have glimpses of the walls of the city, the city Marco Polo seven centuries ago hailed as "a very great and fine city." I can tell it is no longer such a fine place. According to Marco Polo, Kublai Khan's favorite son maintained a magnificent palace here, "with splendid halls, and many chambers, all painted and embellished with work in beaten gold." Not a fleck remains. Only "the massive and lofty wall, ten miles in compass, well-built, and all garnished with battlements" has endured—but it's enough. The city walls of Xi'an—forty feet high, fashioned from rammed earth and brick, the old archers' towers intact—transfix me.

I want a closer look, but before we can reach the city gate, we veer south to a more modest gate in more modest walls, just a dozen feet high. At a horn beep—the last of a thousand honks en route—the gatekeeper emerges from his house and ushers us onto campus. My apartment proves to be one of seventy in a complex that looks twenty years old; in fact, it was erected two years ago by a construction brigade of peasants, according to Professor Zhong, who insists on hauling my trunk up the three flights. He's twice my age, but I let him have his way.

As for my living quarters: the door is held in place by a nominal lock. Inside it's stark, all concrete. There's no beaten gold, no detail work at all. In the kitchen a cold water tap drips into the depths of a cement basin.

The water, Professor Zhong points out, is undrinkable. He fills a three-quart stainless steel tea kettle, screws open the valve of a gas canister on the floor, and, on the third try, fires both self-lighting burners on a shiny new hot plate. Then he rinses my dishes, pans, and chopsticks under the tap, drying each item between his fingers. Be circumspect, he warns me; keep everything clean or risk illness.

On the edge of the sink rests a rag mop with a thick birch handle; it looks to me like a prosthetic clubfoot from a Grimms' fairy tale. The kitchen curtain, a plain sheet, is impaled on a piano wire. Through the curtain I can see my building's double: five stories, seventy balconies, clothes drying on poles. There are blocks and blocks of these modern complexes on campus, and everyone who works here lives within these college walls. We're one big happy work unit.

In the living room, Professor Zhong shows me my two greatest luxuries—a tiny electric refrigerator and a large German color television. The TV is wrapped in a green velvet TV cozy to shield its screen from the daily drift of dust. There are also two overstuffed chairs draped with bath towels and matching antimacassars. My furniture is standard People's Republic issue, including two spittoons. A bare bulb hangs from its cord in the center of the room, low enough to graze me as I rise. I have been issued a thermos, the life-sustaining vessel of China, as ubiquitous as the cuspidor.

In the bedroom is a desk, a standing wardrobe, a narrow bed on a metal frame, and glass doors to a balcony.

And in the hall is the bathroom—a raised closet. The toilet is a ceramic bowl in the elongated shape of a bedpan, set deep into the center of the floor. Professor Zhong demonstrates its use by yanking a chain attached to an overhead tank on the back wall; it delivers a healthy Victorian flush. I have no idea how to approach this hole in the floor, however. Is it ass forwards or ass backwards?

The entire closet also functions as my shower. A heater box is nailed to the side wall. I am to fill the box with a hose routed from the toilet tank, then plug an electrical cord into an outlet. Water heats in about fifteen minutes—plenty of time to undress, cover the toilet bowl with a wooden lattice, stand on it, and crank open the nozzle on the shower head.

After introducing me to my apartment fixtures, Professor

Zhong bids me farewell; he assumes I require my afternoon nap. At dinnertime, he's back, with an immense plate of jiaozi—a northern version of dim sum, often described in the West as steamed dumplings, but dumplings they aren't. His wife has prepared them; she is sorry she can't have me over just now. As it is, I can eat no more than a third of the plate. I place the remainder in the little fridge. I'm without appetite.

Again, Professor Zhong has pressing business; he hands me over to my neighbors across the landing: Fred and Rita, two more American teachers.

Fred and Rita have been here for half a year. They have survived the dry, freezing winter, bundled in mittens and down vests worn, like Walt Whitman's hat, indoors and out. Their sole source of heat has been a stove the size and shape of a large incense burner set in the middle of their living room. It is fed with perforated pucks of coal. Xi'an burns its winter coal until the air turns black and the street markets shrivel into a few stalls selling cabbage by the pile, but spring's arrived, Fred and Rita are thawing out, there's less coal and more fresh produce. They are looking forward with disturbing delight to warm dust storms, summer rains, and streets a foot deep in mud.

The stove pipe, which was routed out through a hole in the living room window, still lies in lengths on the living room floor. I help Fred walk the stove into a corner. We celebrate the arrival of spring with a bottle of harsh Chinese wine. Fred unscrews the cap. Rita pours. She's in her late twenties, lean and short, a fighter—she would be wiry if she were taller—with long dark hair, Germanic face, symmetrical features, all sorts of energy and conviction concentrated there. Rita has just spent four years teaching in Japan with Fred. Before that, Fred lived all over the world, from Turkey to Laos. He began teaching for the Peace Corps and never returned home. He's short, too, and extremely soft spoken, approaching forty, hair catching silver, a New England face, handsome, straight-forward. Turns out to be an ironist, while Rita's the brash one. She spent last week in an oxygen tent with bronchial problems, but that hasn't slowed her down. Fred says he came down with the runs again this morning. Plenty to look forward to, from the sounds of it.

Fred and Rita give me a crash course in surviving Xi'an. It is like hearing two people read aloud from Franz Kafka's diaries. It's clear I'll have to learn everything over: how to mail a letter and park a bike; how to tell a two fen from a five fen note; how to fry peanuts, boil milk, and skin tomatoes; how to buy eggs by the jin, rice by the liang, and beer by the bowl — any transactions to be conducted exclusively in Chinese, all to be learned soon: before tomorrow morning, preferably. By the time they go over it twice, I feel like a child in someone else's house.

When I return to my apartment it's midnight. Having heard that China is overrun with rats, I close the door to the water closet tightly, the door to the living room, too. I hook the bedroom door from the inside. I'm hermetically sealed off from the rest of China. Time to tuck in, alone and palely sagging. My mattress is stuffed with a bare inch of cotton batting, my pillow with the dried husks of beans, hard as kitty litter.

I'm as sleepless as a novice monk. To be exact, I'm weeping. I'm weeping because this is the greatest mistake of my life—coming here. I can not believe I did this. If the bad water and rotten food don't finish me off, then sadness and stupidity will. I am incredibly far from everything that ever mattered, too far to run home. I'm heaving deep down without making a sound, locked up inside this concrete vault.

— : : —

I wake early, fresh, without the slightest kink, fit and finely fettled. For my first breakfast in Xi'an, I boil the two eggs Rita gave me, then meet Fred on the landing and wheel the bike I borrowed from Rita down the stairs. I follow Fred north toward the city.

It's a twenty minute ride to the south wall, but there are lesser walls everywhere surrounding work units—institutes, factories, stores, I can't tell exactly what. The buildings are monotonous, brick or sometimes earthenware with gray-tiled roofs, and all signs, where there are signs, are in Chinese characters. It's wonderfully baffling. I give Fred a running commentary, he just laughs. Women sweep the streets, the dust rises in a cloud and settles back down where it began as soon as the brooms have passed. There are more pack animals than trucks, and even more bicycles, great thickets of bicycles: muscular, black single-speed bikes built to last a lifetime; three-wheeled bikes pedaled by hand for the handicapped; bikes welded to wagons loaded with vegetables or pork flanks heading to market—on every bike a bell, and all the bells tolling at the intersections. Men in uniforms baton the traffic from oval platforms, but they are seldom on duty for long; I spot them chatting near the traffic control booths on every corner. Rototillers tow carts from the communes; peasants in black harness haul wagons of rebar (steel bars used to reinforce concrete), concrete forms, ceramic pots of soy sauce; parents push babies in bamboo prams that look like cribs on wheels . . . and Fred laughs at me in his quiet way until we're trapped behind a shitwagon—that is, a donkey cart with a barrel of human excrement destined for the farm. He tells me that he believes he has been chosen to be behind such a wagon on the day the barrel of night soil comes loose, rolls off, and bursts open in the street. It is his destiny.

Astraddle the barrel, the night soil driver flicks a long cat-o-nine-tails which we duck as we pass. Ahead, the air sweetens. We make good time. Riding a bike in China is like crossing the torrents of a stream on a loose sprinkling of stones. The rhythm and the rule come to me.

At the southern gate to the city, we pass through a forty-foot-long tunnel under the archers' tower where traffic is funneled into Xi'an. The street widens on the other side. We park our bikes at the first traffic circle in the center of Xi'an, where Bei, Nan, Dong, and Xi Dajie—North, South, East, and West Big Streets—intersect, where the Bell Tower has stood, solid and unnailed, for six centuries. Its three tiers of green-glazed roof tiles and soaring eaves flaked in gold are the stuff of feudal China, but radiating outward is a less flamboyant architecture: a modern city of cement.

We cross Dong Dajie to the main post office. The steps are lined with men crouching over bundles of rice paper. They hire themselves out to read and write letters, Fred informs me. He wedges his way through the crowd inside, props his elbows down on the counter, and orders two overseas stamps — 80 fen for a letter, 70 fen for a postcard. Everyone hugging the counter appears to be killing time. They scrutinize us closely. Retreating to an island in the lobby, Fred dips a stick into a glue well and seals an envelope, stamps it and a postcard. Then we struggle back to the edge of another counter. The clerk weighs the letter, nods, hits it with a seal, and sits back down. He is still reading Fred's postcard when we leave.

We head west to the Drum Tower, another six-hundred-year-old Ming monument, pass under it and turn left onto a winding street, too narrow for motor traffic. Children call out to us and follow along. At a small gate, we enter the grounds of the Great Mosque of Xi'an, parts of which date back to the first arrival of Islamic traders in China, 1200 years ago. We find ourselves quite alone at last. Peaceful place, perhaps the only one within the walls of the city.

Outside of the mosque gate, we stroll through the Moslem sector of Xi'an as aimlessly as possible. Fred buys a skewer of boiled lamb. The houses here are built of earth; the floors are of beaten dust. These could be the back streets off the old Silk Road, but somewhere a TV flickers, a shortwave radio blasts Radio Moscow in English. . . . The next generation is on its way. Even the Hui people will be living in subdivisions soon. New winds blow in from the West. Old Xi'an ripens for the leveling. Raze low the gray roof tiles, comrade: the nth modernization is Levittown East.

— : : —

The first week in Xi'an I dissolve into my surroundings, as grim and colorless as they may be. There's no way to forecast the shape of things to come. The clouds from every direction are as tangled as the T'ao-T'ieh, the mythic beast that devours everything in its path.

I find myself delighting in each new deprivation. Already I've lost weight. I add a new notch to my belt. I appear to be starving—I suppose I am starving—yet I grow stronger each day.

The local cuisine is abysmal: the steamed bread is tasteless, heavy, and the pork is not meat at all, but what Rita calls *p.f.*, or pork fat. Our staple is the venerable green vegetable, usually wilted cabbage fried in rice or steamed in envelopes of slick pasta. Rapeseed, the only cooking oil we can procure, is elsewhere reserved for lubricating heavy machinery. It has a raw edge to it, slicing through the stomach lining like a rusty blade.

Professor Zhong visits me seven days in a row. The foreign language division is his fiefdom, he's lured me here, and so he has a vested interest in my good spirits and in my waistline, too. He insists that I come over for breakfast the next day. His building is three past mine. When I arrive, he offers me a seat on his armless couch facing two stuffed chairs. A desk in the living room corner, a small TV draped in silk, bookcases on the walls, plus two bedrooms, a kitchen, a utility room add up to spacious quarters for just a professor, his wife, a son, and a pregnant daughter-in-law. But by my reckoning, Professor Zhong is owed. He tells me without prompting that during the Cultural Revolution his quarters on this campus consisted of a jail cell; mowing lawns and tending pigs comprised his duties. He's not been out of China since I was born, since the revolution. We are alumni of the same university, as it happens: in 1947, he attended college in America, in the town I left. A year later he returned to help rebuild China. In 1966, Professor Zhong was cut off from the English language for ten years. Yet he speaks superb English now, and I can't help liking him. He's curious, self-effacing, and willing to make jokes about himself, but he's cunning. He's had to be. He's well-fed, too. We munch on tea-boiled eggs. I notice they keep two laying hens on the balcony. I stuff myself. His wife insists that I eat more. She serves me a breakfast beer. I turn down nothing.

When I leave, Professor Zhong walks me all the way down to the street, the mark of a formal man. Squinting at me through his black-rimmed glasses, he resembles a raccoon. He appears to be deciphering tiny inscriptions through a magnifying glass; when he reads, he must hold the page scant inches from his eyes. I imagine that this is a legacy of his imprisonment during the Cultural Revolution.

Next week or perhaps the week after, I will undertake my duties as a teacher. My students have arrived—doctors from all over China, each selected by his work unit for a special intensive language course. They all dream of going to America, but tomorrow I must test them and turn half of them away.

From his own savings, Professor Zhong loans me a hundred yuan during the first week—cash he has on hand. When I start teaching, I'll draw five times that much—more than my boss, more, in fact, than any teacher or surgeon in China, more than the President of the Medical College, and for all I know more than Deng Xiaoping. That's how they attract foreign teachers, even though the pay in American currency wouldn't compensate a paperboy.

— : : —

During his latest visit of the week, Professor Zhong proclaims that Americans are much franker than the Chinese. Therefore I must tell him whatever it is I need. I tell him I need nothing more. He presses me. Isn't it true that Americans like carpets? I can hardly deny this proposition. He's satisfied. Wheels turn behind his deep glasses. To date, however, no carpet has shown up at my door.

What I can't tell Professor Zhong is that I would swap any carpet in China for the most mundane impossibility—a direct phone line to the Xi'an Pizza Factory No. 9. . . . "Yes, a sixteen-incher will do. Tomato sauce and mozzarella cheese? Of course. And Canadian bacon, Italian sausage, green peppers— How's that again? Oh sure, just give me the works, comrade. . . . Hold on—someone at the door." I toss the phone down the toilet, which incidentally I can now raise to a sitting height at the touch of a button.

A messenger shatters the door into a heap of perfectly turned chopsticks. He's dressed in the uniform of a French waiter and presents me with a pound of butter on a glass tray. There's a loaf of Wonder bread tied St. Bernard-style around his neck. "It's lucky I found you when I did, sir," he says. "The only reason you're still in existence at all is that you have been able to draw on decades of stored Crisco."

Before I can fleece this waiter of his rare treasures, however, he is trampled by a dozen brassy teenagers in red stripes bearing hamburgers, fries, and chocolate shakes in Styrofoam boxes.

Professor Zhong calls again and again. He unrolls an edible carpet with all the trimmings. I dream that I cannot stop eating. I am dissolving into the wall; I am disappearing down a crack. If I don't find more to eat, I'll swallow myself whole.

— : : —

During my second week in Xi'an, a Brother typewriter arrives on Friday, a Sanyo ghetto blaster on Saturday, and Professor Zhong on Sunday for my second lesson in Chinese. He's been drilling me in simple putonghua (Mandarin) sentences, tone by tone; in return, I lash him with idiomatic English, although he hardly needs it.

Already I've learned to count to ten, to ask prices, to buy. What else is there to know? The rest is a matter of nerve, and I am not short of that. I rehearse all morning, then shove off for the post office to buy stamps. I have borrowed Rita's bike again. She's only been back in the oxygen tent once since my arrival. She's fine today. It's just that every three weeks she falls apart, completely apart. A day later she's running twice the speed of anyone else. I've a racking cough myself, of course, which started the day I arrived. Otherwise, I'm frightfully healthy.

I pedal north, then east, to the post office in Xiaojie, lock my bike at the brick wall, and pay the attendant, who has roped off half the sidewalk, two fen to watch it. I hand my letter to the postal clerk. She weighs it, stamps it with a seal, and nods. In toneless Chinese I ask to buy ten eight-mao stamps. It works like an incantation.

Confident, I walk to the corner, turn left for the free market. The cheapest produce is handled in the bleakest government warehouse—it has the atmosphere of Stalinist Russia. Almost everyone prefers the open air avenue of private stalls. Usually I find at least one new offering: a shipment of small oranges, finger bananas, the first tomatoes, unripened strawberries. I always ignore the hacked up pork, the unidentifiable animal carcasses on the sidewalk, the caged chickens, the tables of vegetables I can't identify, and go behind the stalls to the row of egg sellers, women, mostly old peasants, bent at waist and knee over their baskets. The shit is still on the egg here. Today I withdraw a plastic bag from my shoulder sack, ask one woman her price—eight for a kwai, the kwai being the dollar bill of China (one yuan in renminbi, the local Chinese currency, good in no other nation on Earth). It means that these protein-rich eggs are expensive indeed. I pull eggs out of the straw, hold some to the sky, shake a few near my ear. I can't really tell fresh from rotten, but after observing the careful Chinese shoppers, I can put on a good show. I pick out my eight. The seller has a scale, she sells by the jin, and she places each egg in the woven basket fastened to one end of a calibrated stick. Her hand serves as the fulcrum.

Xi'an, even in these southern suburbs, is undergoing capitalistic sprawl. The avenue of the free vendors is backed on either side by a line of small shops dispensing shoes, utensils, candies, toilet paper, whatever turns up. There's a dentist yanking his quota of bicuspids in one storefront, followed by a bicycle parts shop and two smoky cafes. Everyone has a business license, except perhaps those on the outer fringes who dump their wares on the curb and pack them up in a flash if there's a hint of authority in the air. In the alley behind the shops is a long row of itinerant barbers, cobblers, and seamstresses, hands chock full of straight razors, water pans, wide-handled scissors, and foot-propelled black iron sewing machines.

On my way home from Xiaojie I stop at the corner display of public notices and wanted posters, those civic lessons hung out like wet sheets. There is quite a congregation this time of black-and-white glossies illustrating the results of a life of crime (a criminal slumped over after execution) and of simple carelessness (a bicycle and rider wrapped seven ways around the crumpled grill of an army jeep) — Xi'an's version of *People* magazine.

I dismount at the pedestrian opening in the college's iron gate and walk my bike home, up the three flights, grab the tea kettle, and head back down to the boiler house, a block away. I pass my neighbor, Dr. Fu, second in charge of surgery at the attached hospital. He shares the landing on the third floor with Fred and Rita and me. Dr. Fu is always dressed in the same muscle-man T-shirt. He has superb muscular tone although he could hardly weigh above a hundred pounds. He speaks the most impeccable English on campus. In the evenings I hear Beethoven from his room — a tiny room, less than a bedroom, which makes me feel particularly sheepish since I learned that he resided in my quarters until I arrived. Now he's without a shower, a TV, a refrigerator, and he says he is pleased that he can assist me by moving next door. He is carrying a sheet metal watering can, which he is looking at with amusement. To me he says, "My shower," smiling, shaking his head.

The boiler is a new twelve foot, coal-fired tank housed in a brick shack with five taps routed into the courtyard. It shuts down about midnight, along with the electricity and cold water flow. At five every morning, the utilities are reengaged. The rush of cold water as it is flushed through the vacant pipes at dawn reminds me of some northern god hawking and spitting through the collapsed mouth of the world—a sound like teeth being ground to powder by a treadle drill.

— : : —

The fourth and final American teacher is Rick Wacker, a six foot sixer who speaks Chinese. He turns up on my landing a week after I've met everyone else, talking about how he's been too long in China, two years already, and how it's high time to hightail it back home. Trouble is, he has no idea where he wants to go or what he wants to do when he finally does get around to packing up. America's become an abstract entity, a construction of words and pictures one sees in a magazine of exotic cultures.

Wacker is curious about every object provided for me. I show him my Brother portable manual typewriter with its errant F key. Everytime I strike F, the pad flies off its lever like a hammered Chiclet. Wacker knows this machine and its 44 cousins quite well; he spotted the whole batch of them one morning on a shelf at the post office. They lay in state there, undelivered and unrequested, for six months. A few inquiries indicated that no one at the Medical College had bothered to pick them up. Wacker got the proper signatures and recruited his students to do the pick up. The name Rick Wacker, however, was not on the list of typewriter recipients.

Next he wants to see my shower. His broke last summer and he has used cold water all winter, explaining that it's easier to do that than ask for a repair. Possibly he's right. I offer him a hot shower anytime he wants, but Wacker hasn't taken me up on it yet. He prefers to suffer, in the Chinese way. Every afternoon, he holes up in his fifth-story apartment, studying Chinese, working on his tones in seclusion. When he's in the streets, he looks the least Chinese of any of us — the clean shaven face of Gary Cooper, the tallest person in a city of millions.

The four of us, Fred and Rita, Wacker and me, are always ravenous and on the prowl for new foodstuffs, new restaurants, imported goods we can connive to buy for Chinese money rather than the hard currency (FEC) tourists are issued. Last week Wacker turned up a coffeehouse serving yogurt from ceramic jars and sweet coffee in glasses; there is a hefty deposit on both containers. The owner, with twice too many teeth, looks like Jerry Lewis. The clientele is young and tries to look trendy — plenty of turtlenecks and sunglasses. Across the street is a wonton restaurant where we are seated the next day for lunch — in a back office, as it turns out, at the boss's desk.

Saturday, Fred took us downtown to his favorite, a vegetarian cafe with his coveted Four Dumpling Rating. It's no cleaner or quieter than any other dive and just as difficult to order in, but it always produces the odd dish of dofu shaped to look like the meats we can never find. Beer comes in plastic mugs rather than bowls—the latest rage, it seems. No tea, no rice. Customers are free to spit on the floor and smoke as they sup. It's foul and loud and dirty with bulk beer and peanuts on the chopstick and cabbage-clotted steamed jiaozi sold by the liang, which is about two pounds. The owner even comes forward to welcome us, clearing a particularly foul tabletop of bones and snot with a sweep of his bare arm.

Afterwards, a beggar, wrapped in coal-stained swaddling, drops by. He hovers at our backs, waiting to sit in our place and wolf down any scraps we have rejected. It makes Fred nervous; he's the only one of us with a conscience. Even the beggars in Xi'an must have a city permit—in this case, to beg—Wacker tells us.

And always there's a parade of peasants outside any lousy restaurant we choose, staring intently in at us. We're the number one attraction in downtown Xi'an, big-nosed orang-utans with passports and running shoes. It's a wonderful life. We're rich and famous and skinny at last. Growing skinnier all the time, honored guests at a banquet of ghosts.

SHADOWBOXING WITH RONALD REAGAN

When I awake on Sunday, Xi'an looks every bit like a living tomb, but it is the ancient tombs of the dead which draw visitors today, among them our glorious leader, the President of the United States.

Ronald Reagan's advance party arrived a week ago. A contingent of Secret Service agents occupies the fourth floor of the Renmin Hotel. This is Xi'an's largest and most unfriendly holding tank for foreign visitors; it was engineered by the Russians in the fifties and the Chinese are barred from entering its premises, although the new neon sign reads "People's Hotel of Xian." There was once a stately sign in the main courtyard of the Renmin Hotel proclaiming:

The Force at the Core Leading Our Course Forward Is the Chinese Communist Party—MAO TSE TUNG

It was a large sign, painted red, and one day just last winter two workers with iron mallets arrived and broke it to bits.

Now Reagan's agents, walkie-talkies holstered on their hips, consume the best imported foods the Renmin Hotel can offer and entertain themselves nightly on its off-limits rooftop. Their mission is to establish a complex communications link between central China and the White House. This requires 42,000 pounds of high technology, not to mention a few screwdrivers and wire-strippers. All this so that, should R.R. wish to call home, he need not wait hours for an international operator to make the connection, as the rest of us do. He will merely push a button. The President's six-hour visit to Xi'an will cost us a cool couple million.

Reagan's brief detour to Xi'an has been prompted by his wish to see the terra-cotta army of Qin Shi Huang Di (259–210 B.C.), first emperor of China, builder of the Great Wall, burner of books, seeker of immortality. Ten years ago, a portion of this life-sized force, which guards the emperor's tomb and vast underground city, was unearthed, reassembled, and shined up for visitors. It has put Xi'an squarely on the map of mass tourism.

Last week I paid my own visit to these same clay warriors that have lured an American president. Professor Zhong arranged a place for me on a busload of officials from the Ministry of Health in Beijing; they were in town on a sightseeing junket. The clay army was our last stop. Our first stop predated even the first emperor of China. It was Banpo, where the Stone Age dead have been scraped out of their death holes and slender funeral urns, reassembled, and tossed into dark display cribs. Banpo was possibly the driest and most dismal major exhibit on Earth: eight thousand years of compressed dust, gray as brain matter—the color of soil after it had utterly died.

From Banpo, our bus roared through village after village of mud and straw. Peasants crouched at the edge of the road—it might as well have been the edge of the world— stoking long reed pipes, faces dark, beards wisps of white. Man and earth are still close here. The ends of empires and of entire eras of civilization have never made a difference. We were traveling on Sao Mu, the Feast of the Dead, and the dead were everywhere—in the houses, in the fields and hills, in the faces along the way which were the faces of Qin. We cut across the tumuli of the old dynasties of China which radiate outward from Xi'an in concentric bands. Most of the burial mounds we passed on the way had never been opened. They made up the thousand hills—the fallen constellations— of the low, flat Wei River plain.

The most prominent burial mound was Emperor Qin's own, the Great Pyramid of China. Although Emperor Qin's armies and steeds have now been unearthed, his actual tomb is still closed—a rounded heap of earth a hundred feet high, a quarter mile wide at its base. When we pulled over for lunch on the flanks of Li Shan, Black Horse Mountain, I could see the tumulus of Emperor Qin on the plain, like the breast of a recumbent goddess. Our driver, finishing a liter of Xian Beer, tossed the big bottle out the window. I heard it smash on the roadside.

When Qin Shi Huang Di reached the throne at age thirteen, the preparations for his death had commenced here, concluding with his death at age forty-nine. In life, Qin presided over the first unification of China; regulated the written language, the currency, the weights and measures, even the span of cart axles; burned books, persecuted intellectuals and completed the Great Wall; but his greatest achievement was his city of the dead, of which only a few boulevards near the outer wall are exposed today.

Building a city for the dead had been the paramount task of the Qin dynasty. The prime minister was in charge, the leading general supervised the site, and 700,000 workers were conscripted to dig, haul, hammer, fire, and finish the city on the plain. Because it was filled with nothing but inanimate, often life-size statuary and artwork, this was a city greater and more enduring than any of its contemporaries, greater than Athens, greater than Rome. Qin's tomb was merely the innermost chamber. The underground city was surrounded by an inner wall, two and a half miles in circumference, and an outer wall, larger still. Between these walls, a full mile east of Qin's tomb, a peasant brigade from the Xiyang People's Commune hauled up the first terra-cotta head 2,184 years later.

Our bus rolled on from the sealed tomb of the emperor across this city of the dead, buried under the plains east of Xi'an, to the open vaults of the clay army. We straddled the center line, passing carts and animals, bikes, and rototillers, our driver hitting the horn hard, creeping up on the far side of other buses, trucks, and red-flag limousines, then snapping us back at the last possible moment to avoid a head-on collision. In this way we were carried out of the age of stone, through iron and copper and bronze, into concrete and finally all the way to titanium, arriving at the terra-cotta vaults, one of the great archaeological sites of the century.

It proved to be no more than the Mount Rushmore of China. Here the endless busloads of tourists, as many from China as anywhere else, were funneled through ticket booths into an arching and ugly stadium—no cameras allowed. The souvenir shops sold tons of slides and colored pictures on the outside. Inside, the excavations were a disappointment. I had expected a mile walk through rubble and an open place in the earth; instead, I was delivered to a Circus Maximus of Scientific Realism.

The furrows in which Qin's army stands today are little changed, but the heavens are neither of earth or sky—they are of corrugated steel. The crowds push in from the rails on three sides. I enter the enormous shed and look down from the sidelines onto the streets of the First Emperor's army, paved in blue brick.

The assumption is that the emperor ordered that his entire army be cast in terra cotta and stationed to defend the outer walls of his eternal city. Three of the vaults have been explored so far; only the first, the largest, the one the tourists see, remains open. Here, the heroic, individualized soldiers and steeds march in long ranks to the east through eleven parallel corridors of rammed earth. As one particularly painful guidebook for visitors exults:

These figures, lifelikely shaped and colorfully painted, are of high artistic value. Over 6,000 clay warriors could be assumedly unearthed from this pit if it would be completely excavated. This would be really an artis-

tic reappearance of hundreds of Qin Shi Huang's warriors. With its artistic momentum, it could be acclaimed
a piece of great masterwork.

I've no idea what artistic momentum is; the momentum for
this monument was clearly not the spin of life, but the
gravitational force of death. It's a grand site—and entirely
lifeless.

Here was China's oldest crossbow; here, its first brick
wall. The paint, which has been scorched, eroded, and
peeled away from the terra-cotta figures, once provided a
unifying element. The mineral dyes were bold and bright the
day they were applied. The soldiers were not so gray then.
Their generals were robed in green; the infantry wore shiny
black armor; and the nostrils, mouths, and ears of their
steeds were red as blood, their teeth and hooves white as
limestone. All these bright monuments were lowered into
these walled ditches and covered over with ceiling timbers,
mats, and a foot of loess and planting soil.

These warriors are quite tall for Chinese, none less than
1.75 meters. The generals stand over six feet and wear
double-tailed caps, war robes, and square shoes turned up at
the toes. The ordinary soldiers—archers, swordsmen, mili-
tia, and charioteers—are clad in scaly armor so finely sculpted that the head and stem of each nail is distinct. Their faces
are stylized but distinct, too, down to the trim of an individual mustache. The horses are magnificent, some saddled,
some bunched in fours to draw the chariots, all vigorous—
teeth straining, necks bolting, manes flying—short-legged
and strong like the steeds seen to this day in provinces west of

Shaanxi. Thirty-eight files of infantry, alternating with chariots and flanked on all sides by archers, form a defense of Qin's tomb to the west. "If it attacked the enemy troops," the guidebook assures us, "it would be very much like throwing a mighty weight upon the birds' eggs." The weapons are real, still sharp, and the arrowheads contain fatal levels of lead.

The most interesting specimens, however, are those not yet assembled: the disembodied heads, arms, hooves, and raiments still imprisoned in the dust, interrupted in their return to the clay—floating to the surface like the wrecked city of Atlantis—pleading to be rejoined, and animated anew by artisans twenty-two centuries after burial.

Perhaps little has changed in those centuries. Certainly the acts of the First Emperor were repeated by the last emperor, Chairman Mao, when he unified a nation, established new standards, burned books, slaughtered scholars, and cast out all reminders of previous regimes; and just as Qin sealed China from the barbarians with his Great Wall, so has Mao. Yet neither tyrant was four years in his grave when everything was reversed. Qin lies under the earth in the center of the old capital, returning to dust; Mao, under glass in the heart of Beijing, waits to be picked apart and scattered to the winds.

Long dreaming of this place, then finally seeing it as I did, I found that I preferred the dream. In the dream I could strip back all the layers and undress the plain; I could stroll among its jade palaces, paved streets, and garden walls; I could tarry in the corridors with that motionless army, a million strong.

Heading home, the walls of Xi'an rose on the horizon like the cliff of an endless rift. For the first time, I began to understand where I was. The First Emperor made two capitals: one above, one below; one for the living, one for the dead. Today the two capitals have merged.

For a thousand years, from the Fall of Rome to the Renaissance, China was the most powerful nation on earth, but remote as Atlantis and as unreal, its very existence reaching the West in a whisper. Even its capital was nameless. An ancient passage from the West, the fabled Silk Road, ended at the gates where, in the midst of level emptiness, stood the largest and the grandest city in the world. Today, the edges of this metropolis have hardened into Xi'an.

Reduced to provincial status and a few million citizens, Xi'an is pitched like a long low tent of ash on an immense plain of fine loess. Encased in high walls of peeling earth, the city is composed entirely of dust. Dust penetrates the thickest enclosures, settles everywhere, and coats everything—the wide avenues, the monotonous new apartment complexes that look thirty years old the moment they go up, the donkey carts, the manure wagons filled by hand from the outhouses. At first glance, Xi'an has no color at all, except gray—gray on its new buildings, its old, slate-roofed houses, its streets paved and unpaved.

Each dawn is masked in a dust so fine the air cannot sift it clear. The great dynasties are entombed about the city in raised mounds of earth like captured moons, motionless and monumental, and the ancient capital is worn into the plain.

— : : —

This morning it is Reagan's turn to survey the remains of China's first emperor, but I'm not much concerned with

Reagan for the moment. Another old man captures my attention. He lives in the corner apartment opposite my complex, next to the wall where garbage is heaped in an open stall. He speaks enough English to tell me he attended college in Tennessee in the thirties. His chief pleasure is shadowboxing at sunrise. I watch his formal movements from my window, curiously private in a culture lacking a word for privacy: measured and precise, unhurried, sharp and limber. Compare him to the latest visitor from the West who comes with his own version of homegrown xenophobia, the pitchman for Death Valley Days, who has already lectured his hosts on God and the Free Economy.

I'm not the least bit curious about how the Chinese will react to Reagan. I know there'll be no reaction in Xi'an, at any rate. No cowboys on TV here. No one in the streets knows Ronald Reagan's name, and America is merely the word for a distant, pretty land.

Sunday, moreover, is the one day off each week, meaning people will be occupied with matters closer to hand: shopping for the week's rice and grain, taking children to the park, donating a day's labor to public works. Life is a series of basic tasks. At most, an American president is a sideshow. So is any foreigner. Within the walls of this city I can ring myself with onlookers simply by standing still; I can be followed for blocks by gawking strangers. In China, all Americans are truly equal—except, perhaps, Reagan himself, who arrives in his own plane, lands on time in Beijing with all his luggage and, with 600 attendants, is never likely to be stranded. His banquets in Beijing and Shanghai would cost ten years' salary for a worker in Xi'an. The entire spread has been broadcast to us on China Television the last few nights, right after we finish our own dinners—the stuff of myth and Middle Kingdom. Insulated from the ruder hints and assaults of the lives of the masses, world leaders need not boil their own drinking water.

The vaults of Emperor Qin are closed, even to foreign tourists, this Sunday. No doubt quite a few groups were bumped. Never mind. The first are doomed to be the last to truly see. I had hoped that Reagan would at least have to travel those few miles east of Xi'an where one is dropped into the well of time: mud villages and villagers unmarked by the press of twenty-three centuries; molded clay, still fresh and living along the roadside, watching strange caravans pass today as they have always passed on the road to the capital; sights enough to singe the modern senses, to rearrange a Western vision of the world and pack it into a crease reptilian in its intensity. But these sights—rural China, the poor Shaanxi heartland—Mr. Reagan has been spared: a new highway, paved by hand and bypassing the more primitive villages, opens for the first time today to serve his grand motorcade.

The peasants who remain alongside the new thoroughfare have been ordered to stay inside. In the courtyard of the terracotta armies, a mock free market has been orchestrated to entertain the first lady and the press. In short, everything's been dressed up, and a trip to the tombs today resembles a ramble to Arlington, Virginia, rather than to Tijuana, Mexico. The Qin tombs have become fully emblematic of China today, of a deliberate reassembly of the past in order to play the modern game: attract foreigner visitors and hard cash to the table, then convert the take into advanced technology. Reagan's here to prime the pump. He won't even enter the city walls of Xi'an.

At midnight the dust lifts from the streets and there is a momentary transparency of vision, even of idle thought, in my cement room. I'm thinking of the Secret Service boys in the Renmin Hotel, of the twenty-one tons of computer parts packed in metal cases in the backs of trucks, of the unlimited personal luggage piled outside their doors on the fourth floor which the porters will haul off at dawn. The billiard table, the barbecue, and the leftover ballpark franks they brought with them to China are crated up now. The million-dollar telephone has been ripped out of the wall. At dawn, the old shadowboxer reappears in the courtyard, a hot dog in one hand, a phone in the other.

OF CABBAGES
AND PORK FAT

onight we go around the corner for dinner. Rita brings the chopsticks. A loud and lousy worker's joint, the only niceties are real tablecloths, a bit oily, slick and spotted like walrus skins; otherwise, beer from a bowl and lumps of jiaozi. Fred does order one Wei River trout, bones in, but it seems a little rancid; nobody touches it.

Then we're off to the provincial opera. Admission five mao. We get nonconsecutive seat numbers so that we are sprinkled through the auditorium in a salad of peasants smelling of garlic. Everyone converses nonstop. Shaanxi is no-frills opera at its most operatic with liberal helpings of masks and gongs and two-man tigers eluding paper swords. I feel at home packed between whole families. After an hour of incomprehensible spectacle, we make for the exit in unison, cross the main avenue, and buy dixie cups of soft ice cream.

Our social life in Xi'an is looking up. Last night Professor

Zhong garnered us tickets to a performance of Xi'an's famed T'ang Dynasty Dancers. The theater was a tad ritzier than the local opera. The block was littered with air-conditioned buses because the performance was always booked by foreign tour groups. The audience, in fact, happened to be made up of 200 American beef farmers from Kansas who'd spent the day on a whirlwind inspection of the seven most scintillating sites of Xi'an, from Emperor Qin's pastures to the Big Wild Goose Pagoda. The women wore real pearls, their faces glazed with makeup and blush, and their husbands clutched two or three long-snouted Leica cameras which they wielded like ball cutters. As the scarved dancers streamed across stage, the audience jumped up and down; their flashbulbs popped like hot butterfat, smearing the silken veils in yellow. It looked like a cheap disco.

Surrounded by my compatriots for the first time in months, I felt like a foreigner in their midst. I couldn't wait to get away.

: : ▬

The foreigners who have it the worst are black: a dozen students from the Middle East and Africa—mostly from Sudan, in fact, so we refer to them collectively as the Sudanese. They start off with a year of intensive Chinese language study in Beijing; then it's four straight years of engineering classes in Xi'an. They hole up together in a special dormitory. Few of them have daddies or governments rich enough to spring for vacations abroad, so Xi'an is like a four year jail sentence without furlough. In China's provinces especially, black men are so alien they hardly even

39

figure in mythology, so what the Sudanese are forever experiencing is beyond deliberate racism; it's curiosity, wonder, and shock. When they board the bus for a trip together, the Chinese get off and stare back in.

They're all Moslem, too, so few of them drink or smoke openly. They play it cool, except for Raoul. Raoul's a Middle-Eastern showboater who looks like a carpet salesman. He belongs in Soho or Las Vegas, surrounded by floozies and tanker trucks full of Johnnie Walker Red. In Xi'an, he teases Chinese students, shopgirls, and waitresses into being called his girlfriends, and he smuggles liters of the local vodka into the best hotel lounges. He always puts a pack of Marlboros on the table before he sits down. Once an hour he draws one of us aside, sighs deeply, shakes his head, and compresses his entire lament into a single all-telling expletive: "China!"

Raoul is never going to let us forget what a hideous hole we've fallen into. "China—shit!" But he's formed an escape plan: he means to drink himself to death. I never see him not drinking. He can drink anyone else under several tables. So I should have been more careful when I ran into him at the Friendship Store Cafe this morning: wouldn't have ended up pie-eyed, anyway. What the hell: we split a six-pack of Tsing Tao, rode down the middle of main street, south to the Binguan, passed a few more hours in the bar, then joined the Sudanese for a set dinner. From there down the hall to another bar.

I felt quite low about everything Chinese under Raoul's dissection, even though I think I love China—love it in a way he won't accept for a second. Twice Raoul's companions tried to drag him out of the bar. He laughed at them, called them fools, blew smoke in their faces. Later he tried to sell his ghetto blaster to the bartender for foreign currency, a criminal offense. Not that he cared.

"Let them string me up," he said, "just so they send me home afterwards, because this is the most backward, nasty, stupid, unenlightened, smug, two-faced, idiotic waste of civilization ever devised; the worst disaster since the disappearance of the dinosaur. China? China!"

The last thing I remember, before the glass of vodka snapped in midair between my fingers, was Raoul unbuttoning his polyester shirt as he sat on the bar stool. "Double heart surgery at twenty-one," he said nonchalantly, showing me the scar which divides his chest like a trench.

— : : —

My two most ruthless students, doctors from Canton, hate the food in Xi'an more than I do; succumbing to their wiles, I agree to bankroll a banquet. At six in the morning, we catch the first bus to the central market.

Dr. Lu, age forty, possesses a mean, deprived look, and is the boldest of the class: he asks favors, complains about assignments, and begs me for cast-off books and maps without the least embarrassment. His sidekick, Dr. Li, is much younger and more reserved, shrewd enough to know that if he keeps his mouth shut, he has time to advance—maybe even go abroad. They stick together, Li and Lu, and the other students leave them alone.

No wonder. I watch them attack the market with the precision of archaeologists in the field, winnowing out only the choicest vegetables. I shell out renminbi like a godfather. They pick out pounds of beef and pork and plenty of ginger root. The most delicate decision concerns the chickens—the two roosters. Hens are out of the question; the males are the more tender sex, having escaped the hard labor of laying. Li and Lu determine the age of each prospect by the relative darkness of the claws and preponderance of wrinkles. The two finalists are tied at the ankles and carried home on the bus upside down.

For lunch, the doctors whip together a blitz soup of long noodles, onion, ginger, pork, cabbage, and soy, which we inhale like open drains. Then, as it is naptime, Li and Lu go back to their dorm, dumping the two live roosters on my kitchen floor.

The afternoon mercury rises to about ninety-nine, but the roosters never complain; like me, they are waiting for the slaughter, the plucking, and the gutting. Rita takes one look in my kitchen and disappears.

Dr. Lu, the senior surgeon, is elected to do the cutting, while young Dr. Li, holding each rooster by its heels over a rice bowl, will collect the blood. The necks are quickly slit with the vegetable chopper, the blood refrigerated, the carcasses defeathered and washed in the laundry pan. They wash every part and segment, inside and out—even the intestines, which they plunge with a chopstick. Then they break my heart. They seize my pint of peanut oil, which I have been doling out in place of rapeseed oil—one of only two pints of peanut oil which I know to exist in all of Xi'an. (The other belongs to Rita; she spotted it being sold from a cart.) This holy pint, with which I have previously anointed my pans in a faint mist, they seize and, in an act of culinary insanity, empty completely, half a cup here, half a cup there.

The temperature in my kitchen continues to rise all afternoon. Li and Lu stir some rooster guts into an egg base, dump them into a red hot skillet, shred this omelette into long strips which they toss into a soup pot, along with an expensive fungus called Silver Ear. They roll everything in fresh ginger, even the vegetable entrees, which we begin to eat at about six: a long parade of onions and beans and strips of beef and fried rice with pork. The main bulk of the roosters they boil meanwhile, according to age—seven minutes for these guys. Then they immediately hack them willy-nilly into a thousand pieces and serve them that way, severed and naked. It is like eating the bones of a jigsaw puzzle. Finally comes the coup de grace: blood soup. The congealed rooster blood, cut into squares, floats to the top, and Rita and even Fred demur. Actually, it's tasty. Li and Lu slurp up the whole production, then lean back with grins as wide as Jack the Ripper's. We all down mao tai and Xi'an beer and Rita talks so fast that Li and Lu are baffled.

Later, around midnight, I turn on the blank TV screen and pretend it is snowing outside, too. All over China there is cool snow raining down, cool as a kitchen floor. I turn off the oscillating fan, strip down to nothing, lie back on my hard pillow, and stretch out on the bamboo mat like a fat turtle.

The next day, Rick Wacker returns from a disastrous field trip to Taiyuan, where he insisted on staying with his students in the hotel for Chinese and nearly got kicked out of town. We're glad to see him. He's our main source of the latest campus gossip, in part because he speaks Chinese, in

43

part because his class consists of the older cadres who know all the scandals. This week he's been reading the campus chalkboard where the messages are usually embroidered with hand-drawn flowers, but now there are no decorations, only the plain story of a graduate student and his undergraduate lover. It was discovered that she was pregnant, and he killed himself. Plenty of birth control in China, but none for the unmarried. Wacker adds to this the rumor that our leading expert on traditional Chinese medicine, a rising star with a textbook in English covering everything from ground reindeer antlers to moxibustion, has been caught in the act with a student in his office—he, atop his desk, about to swoop down heroically, she, naked in one corner, waiting with wild eyes. We're dubious about the details of the second story.

Rita persuades Wacker to partake of the leftovers of our already legendary Sunday dinner; then she hands him a plate containing the claws, beak, coxcomb, and eye of a rooster— too strange even for Wacker.

Good thing he abstained. By nightfall the rest of us are bent double with the runs and shivers. I can barely roll over on my back. When the water's turned on at 5:30 in the morning, I just flush down the splatters of the night. Then it's time to crawl across campus to teach. Later, at 2:30, I also have to spend three hours doing Professor Zhong a favor: reciting into a tape recorder the text of his latest manual on English for Chinese medical students. The passages are lifted from an American anthology, via Singapore. After the session, Professor Zhong hands me two vials of herbal pills to cure a stomach cold. They don't work. Suddenly, I remember

44

chancing upon a clipping a few days before departing for China—apparently the first news from Xi'an to filter into an American newspaper in two years:

FLEAS CARRYING KILLER FEVER

PEKING (AP)—A killer fever carried by fleas or lice on rats has afflicted parts of the ancient capital of Xian, foreign residents and travelers from that city reported Monday. Xian, one of the planned stops for President Reagan when he visits China in April, is about 550 miles southwest of Peking. The illness is characterized by high fever, aching joints, and hemorrhaging of blood vessels. It is transmitted by fleas or lice that live on rats.

This provides a cheery picture of Xi'an, not the capital of an empire, but the center of a plague born by lice and fleas astride the backs of rats, as on chariots. Hardly a week in Xi'an, I saw my first rat. Some children were gleefully chasing it around the corner of our building. The parents stood by, laughing and urging the children on. Later I discovered that the Medical College itself is located at the heart of this epidemic—there were a dozen or more campus victims of the plague last year, men under forty. There is no known treatment. The plague of Xi'an begins like a cold, and a few days later your blood vessels are popping and even lockjaw is regarded as a blessing. One day you melt down into your pillow and return to the belly of the earth, where you find Mao white as marble saluting the East and Ronald Reagan lip-synching a press conference to the West, sponsored by twenty-mule team borax.

It's a fever like no other—probably the plague. I drive myself through the center of the earth and wake, like the dead from long sleep, in the middle of the Middle Kingdom, utterly lost inside another body whose hands are formed from an alien dust.

Fortunately, Dr. Fu rescues me. He insists on serving me morning, noon, and night, stuffing me with soups and gruels he prepares himself. I'm too weak to protest. Apparently it isn't enough that I took over his apartment and bike; he also has to act as my nurse.

We've come to know each other pretty well, Fu and I. As the number two surgeon, he has risen to the top of the hospital staff, but his refusal to join the Party leaves him as powerless as an orderly. He can't always schedule surgeries or decide which patients need treatment—those can be political decisions, made by non-doctors. Much of our talk is about who lives and who dies in Xi'an.

As I get better, Dr. Fu talks more about himself. He makes it clear that the number one goal in his life is to leave Xi'an. He simply wants to join his wife in Shanghai. She was given permission to leave two years ago because the air of Xi'an was destroying her lungs. Unfortunately, Dr. Fu is not so unfortunate. Even if he had an ailment, he'd be too good to let go. He's the one all the cadres in town depend on when they need treatment—literally, their backdoor doc, the one they insist upon, even though he despises them.

Lately, Fu has taken to insulting them to their faces. Nearly every evening, campus doctors call on him at home, hoping to cool him off. Fu tells me there's no chance of that. He won't shut up. "There's nothing more that they can do to me. I want to be with my wife, they won't let me go. They want to promote me to Chief of Surgery. They think that's what I want, but what are they giving me? I'll have no power. It's a mockery." When doctors from the West visit Xi'an at Fu's invitation, he has to pay for their stay out of his own salary—from which he can't afford a single medical textbook from abroad anyway. "For twenty-five years I escaped the general misery," Fu says. "Now it's come for me with a vengeance."

Thursday afternoon Fu drops over because he has refused to attend a political meeting at the hospital. He has just put in for a formal transfer to Shanghai. "Only this time, I let them know I'm serious," he says. "I told them if you don't release me now, I'll kill myself."

I ask if they believe him, because I don't. He says that they'd better, because he *is* serious. But what about your wife? I ask. Dr. Fu says they have a pact. This is not the way to do it at all, I insist, but Fu refuses to reconsider. He seems utterly set on this course. Rita's of the opinion that it's romantic nonsense. Fred calls it a calculated bluff. Wacker sees it as the declaration of a desperate man, saying, "He's just tough enough to do it, you know."

— : : —

The new Guest House behind my apartment complex is not completed yet, but is already occupied. I have an excellent view of it from my bedroom terrace. Rick Wacker remembers that there has been at least one major false start: the first two floors had to be leveled and a new foundation poured for some reason he could never determine. Then one morning, when the structure was nearly complete, he noticed that all the toilets and sinks were plummeting from the windows to the courtyard below. This time, there was an explanation: it had been decided that foreigners did not like the fixtures facing the bathroom door; so everything was ripped up and tossed out, new appliances were ordered, the entire building was redone.

The purpose of the new Guest House is to accommodate foreign visitors—doctors, nurses, administrators, for the most part—in splendor, while extracting heaps of hard currency in return. The Guest House is to have its own dining room, cleaning staff, and real hot water piped into every room.

A while back we paid a midnight inspection tour and found four miserable floors of dark, cavernous rooms; the usual incomplete finish work; the shabby white- and green-washed walls. The Guest House looked like a worn-out state institution before it even opened. There were carpets, to be sure, red and brown shag, but no sweepers or vacuum cleaners or steam units, and the rugs were already beginning to stink. The hot water hadn't quite been delivered, either. If it ever is, you can bet it will come out of the tap at 200 degrees.

Nevertheless, doctors and hospital administrators from America began to arrive in small groups as soon as the last toilet was cinched down. Few of them have stayed more than a night; most demand to be moved to a real hotel. The sole exception has been Karl, corporate executive officer of a hospital services complex in Montana. He is content to hole up in his room on the top floor of the Guest House and read paperback science fiction. Usually he's the only guest. Sometimes visiting experts swing by on lecture tours, or surgeons come to demonstrate the latest techniques from the West, and Karl will wine and dine them dutifully at downtown hotels. Once a week or so, he gives lectures on campus about the fundamentals of modern hospital management—an odd curriculum in a system where uncertified cadres rule the roost and patients, if they have enough pull to get in, often wait months in the hospital for a routine operation. Karl seems fazed by nothing; he's on sabbatical leave for three months and quite content to shut himself up in Xi'an, so long as his supply of science fiction holds up.

Professor Zhong has arranged for us to buy meals for half-price at the Guest House whenever we wish. Since even at these rates we have to shell out two kwai, we seldom resort to the first-floor dining hall. Breakfast is the most difficult to resist; there, we hog down entire loaves of real baked bread and butter. We eat like the starved, the rescued. Karl, who is usually the only other diner, sits in the same room but behind a movable screen. We usually go over and sit with him for a while, but Karl is as dull as paste, really. He has no desire to venture out with us into Xi'an. He prefers, he says, to mark time. Karl's sole complaint is that a second trunk, loaded with still more science fiction, has been held up in Shanghai, and try as he may, despite every sort of assurance down the line, he can not get it forwarded to Xi'an. Even the new Land Rover which an American relief organization has donated to the medical college arrives ahead of Karl's trunk, despite the fact that this vehicle had to be fetched in Hong Kong by one of our drivers, driven across the border and seventeen different provinces, each with its own entry regulations and gas ration coupons.

Fortunately, Karl proves to be a soft touch for Rita, who is trying to exchange Chinese money for hard currency for the vacation she and Fred will be taking this summer. She's had a run of piss-poor luck lately with tourists filing in and out of the hotels; their guides have probably warned them that renminbi is hard to spend, except on the streets, and possesses zero cash-in value back home. Karl really doesn't care about all that. He tells Rita he means to spend renminbi at the Guest House, no matter what they say. After all, he's their only full-time guest.

As for Karl's trunk, none of us believes that it will ever reach Xi'an . . . lost, like nearly everything else bearing our remote address, in transit or perhaps still taking up space in a baggage car forgotten on a siding, surrounded by a century of unclaimed packages from the twilight zone.

The only commodities that get through are cabbage and pork fat, heaped in mounds along the streets like rotting tumuli.

SPIRIT WAY

One Sunday morning at the end of spring the four of us bicycle south through the suburbs. The main road divides at an insane asylum and rises for a mile or more to a plateau of wheat fields. We're looking for the stone animals and excavations Fred and Rita spotted in the middle of winter. It's a hot day. Fred and Rita fall back at the rise, dismount, and push their bikes uphill. Even Wacker gives up here, but I keep riding. The more I sweat, the harder I push. My muscles ache to rest—I feel them stretched tight against the bone—but I pedal to the top.

I stop beside the banks of a muddy pool sunk into bare ground. A dozen peasant women and children are washing dishes and laundry here. White and red checked, the village laundry lies on the earth to dry, spread out like enormous postage stamps. At the edge of the fields beyond the pool a row of tall skinny trees like chopsticks have been driven into the ground to break the wind. In the far flats beyond I see the terraced pyramid of a royal burial mound. In a field before it are the heads of stone animals. They stand among green stalks of wheat.

We reach them by pushing our bikes along a rutted path into the fields. The figures form a Spirit Way to a tomb of raised earth, but that ancient road has been erased by the farmers. The statues mark the two sides of the old buried road: first the stone horses, saddled and bridled; then the robed and turbaned guardians, ten feet tall, each clutching an enormous sword in both hands. Their hands meet at the navel; their sword points turn down into the earth.

Walking between statues, we mount the stone horses and stare up at the long faces of the sentinels. They appear to be figures from the T'ang dynasty, but who they were and what they guarded has been forgotten. To the south are the tiled roofs of the village commune. To the north, at the end of this Spirit Way, is the earthen dome with its arched entryway, which the farmers are using as a storage cellar. To the east, a dozen more burial mounds protrude from the wheat fields like swollen bellies. Some of those mounds are a hundred feet high. Most are terraced in grass and wheat. None has been opened except by robbers.

We park our bikes and follow a path to the summit of the royal burial mound: a perfect spot for lunch. We drop our shoulder bags and sit on the hard ground between bunches of quack grass. It is a knoll like any other on the globe, except it has been heaped high by mound-builders to cap a royal grave. Rick Wacker cracks the first of three hard-boiled eggs and breaks into a verse of "Red River Valley." We join in, mangling the lyrics, tossing in Chinese phrases. Fred launches into a discourse on the privies of the world, from Laos to Timbuktu, reminding me of the public outhouses of Xi'an, ventilated sheds every block or two, and the one in the building on campus, where I teach and my seventeen students live, which for some reason is the most odoriferous lavatory I've ever been near.

We're sleepy. No one is ready to move on. Napping is a habit I'll carry back with me if I ever reach America. Wacker lays down like a massive Gulliver, cups his head in his hands, and closes his eyes against the soft blue sky.

I fall half-asleep and dream of red envelopes. A messenger in Imperial T'ang robes trudges to the top of the tumulus and presents us with the envelopes; they are stuffed with pearls and rare jade, worth a hundred million or so on the world market. We vow never to teach baby English again. We vow to dine forever on pure pizza and steak. No more dofu. No more rocky rice. No more steamed bread. No pig fat or cabbage ever again. Fred and Rita sign a ninety-nine year lease on an Indonesian isle, their own Bali with unbreakable indoor plumbing and a waterfall of hot potable water that runs twenty-four hours a day. A place where, Fred claims, everything is always absurd and nobody cares. There they raise a family. Wacker is indecisive. Even with sudden wealth, he has no fixed address, just a wagon which follows him across seven continents. All he requires are dozens of pairs of size thirteen cotton shoes and a portable cold-water sink. No one retires to Xi'an; the notion of Xi'an as a place for retirement does not exist, even in dreams. For myself, I'm content with a cottage of wattles and plywood on the middle finger of Hua Shan, the holy mountain of Northwest China, where I can gaze out all my days on an endless pilgrimage.

Money makes no difference finally, has nothing to do with what we want. What we want is to be in and of the procession, devoid of anxiety and desire, to move and savor and not to think of any end. The messenger takes the envelopes back, unopened, and delivers them into the mansions of the earth, leaving us what we want: all the time in the world today. The lines of wealth, of fame, of family are broken in our palms, but those of luck and life are long; however faint, these are the only lines worth reading from beginning to end.

When we wake, we find royal mounds radiating out across a checkerboard of fields. We hike back down to our bikes and set out for a fresh excavation we spotted from above. A field has been opened up and a foot or more of yellow soil neatly stripped away. Approaching, we can see the foundations of a dozen buildings, their walls long ago broken down, carved out as if by a jackknife. Within those foundations are the bricks and passageways of ancient basements and secret chambers, firepits and altars to house and town gods. On the far edge of the dig a massive white pup tent is pitched. When we near it, a watchman pops out and waves us away. The ground is littered with relics—broken tiles, edges of carved stone, the ruins of another city in the earth. At eye level, it is as barren as the moon.

We wheel away and come out on a dirt road running north to Xi'an. In the fields on the edge of a village, the harvested wheat is being threshed by a donkey hitched to a stone spool. Two children run up to inspect us—a girl and her brother.

The girl's long hair is tied with a red ribbon into a ponytail. When we speak, they bolt.

Near the village we pass an old woman walking in the middle of the street, breasts bared. She doesn't see us. Down a side street we have a quick glimpse of two lovers on a bench, the girl spread-legged on the boy's lap, both looking over the other's shoulder into space.

The village is composed of mud and brick and tile; even the main street is packed clay. The barber is at work on the curb; sleeves rolled up, straight razor in hand, he scrapes away the last hairs of a bald customer seated on a wicker stool, covered neck to ankle in a square white sheet. A water basin, shaped like the black rim of a car wheel, occupies its own stool. All the tools of the trade—brushes, scissors, and straps, wooden combs, and slate mirrors, hang from a bamboo pole.

We stop at the center of the village. Everyone comes out to see us. Mothers hold up their babies. Young men in T-shirts and Mao jackets or army fatigues scrutinize us grimly. Girls in red and pink blouses, shod in vinyl thongs, hold onto their friends. We all have a good stare at each other. A man with a sidecar welded to his bicycle pulls over. This sidecar is a four-tiered wire cage holding dozens of ducklings. We talk a bit with him and laugh, until the village, which calls itself San Da, has its fill of us and we head on for the city.

On the dirt road down to Xi'an we are joined by a merchant riding a bicycle welded to a trailer. These contraptions are heavy and difficult to maneuver, but we egg poor Fred into taking a spin. He immediately ends up in the ditch. Wacker keeps it a little straighter. The merchant rides with us, passing us as we all glide downhill. An old man crouches over his wares in the roadbed; he is selling play money to burn for ancestors, wooden prayer wheels, tin medallions, brooms to sweep graves, paper lanterns, and rolls of firecrackers fat as cigars. We keep gliding.

It has turned into exactly the sort of day to make you think you should never leave Xi'an: riding south of the Wild Goose pagodas, not knowing what you'll come across, whether rows of stone animals and the tombs of high officials stranded in a sea of wheat; or a long plain of unopened tumuli, green and terraced; or a picnic atop a grave; or an unnamed excavation with heaps of blue paving stones in the rope-twine pattern, old as the first emperor and still fired today in the kilns of China; or a village of 4000 peasants with no tour buses parked out back; or ducklings on a bike, a mao each, wholesale; or even a dozen frogs in a laundry pond—so loud in the hot afternoon the sound is like a millrace. Finally you arrive back in Xi'an itself, grayest of the gray at twilight, where you stop, exhausted, and shovel in two helpings of plain, cold white yogurt from the jar. It is as though you've burrowed into the earth and come back out, your skin forever stained the color of the earth.

IN THE WALLS
OF THE CITY

The night's dust is suspended in light when I wake. The windup alarm clock summons me at six, but I shut it off. I am late, as usual; I have to hurry to meet my students. I pull up the sheet, tuck it under the thin mattress, and prop up my pillow, a hard sack of bean husks. The sun pours through the worn pink sheet curtaining the bedroom window. The sky is blue, but I can't see the mountains to the south. I pull yesterday's clothing item by item from the desk chair, relocate Voice of America on the shortwave, but don't listen, content with my isolation. Dressed, I unbolt the bedroom door, turn into the hall, and step up into the water closet. Water from the shower box splatters the back of my neck.

The two pint bottles which Rick Wacker delivered at seven are on the landing. I pry off the paper seals with my army knife, empty the milk into a pan, and heat it on the propane hot plate. The milk stirred down into its second boil, I click off the burner and drop a spoon of instant coffee into my cup. I fill it with steaming milk, damming the scum with a chopstick. The two hard-boiled eggs I consume in a half-dozen bites. In the bedroom I arrange the day's lesson, stuff the papers into my black vinyl shoulder bag, and wheel Dr. Fu's black Phoenix bicycle—which is on permanent loan—out onto the landing, then three flights down to the road.

The silt in the road has dried to a hard shell. At the boiler building the campus doctors are lined up with pots and thermoses at iron taps. I dismount and walk my bike through the gate. The gatekeeper sits on a wooden folding chair against the wall, staring into the air, holding a child on his lap. It all begins like any other working day. . . .

Turning south into the flow of buses and bikes, I can see the outline of the Qingling Mountains, still encased in a haze of dust and coal, dividing northern China from the south. At the gate to the eastern campus, I dismount again. Something different, an omen: a cow stands at the gate, its owner leaning against her patchy flanks, asleep.

My classroom is its usual dull self. The chalk disintegrates as I press it into the board. The particles are suspended shoulder high, too fine to settle, and I wheel in a cloud to face the class. I am seven minutes late. All seventeen of my students are in their seats, of course, in concordance with the chart the class monitor presented me on the second day. They shout my formal title in a chorus, these poor doctors my own age who have left their families elsewhere. Seven days a week they study English furiously, by rote and recitation, stuffed into undecorated dormitory rooms without sinks or showers or hot plates. They seldom venture off campus. They live on the first floor, attend class on the third, and afternoons they stroll in pairs across the grassless quadrangles, books in hand, reading aloud.

The morning is heating up quickly. The students remove their green and blue jackets, forming a sea of plain white shirts. All week they have been delivering oral presentations on the cities and scenery of China. From the side of the classroom, arms folded, I grill them once more with questions for which they have not rehearsed correct answers as a group. I end class a half-hour early. As I leave, I notice my students standing around, at sea, forlorn in the undecorated hallway.

The door to Dr. Fu Yi-Man's room is open on our landing when I get back. I stare in. I can hear a Beethoven symphony in the darkness. There is a fifty-pound sack of rice on the threshold, ripped open for the sorting of stones from kernels. Dr. Fu materializes in the opening, clutching his tin watering can. "Would you care for some rice today?" he asks. "I'm just sorting it."

I tell him no and go into my own apartment. He's still determined to go through with the double-suicide. Even Fred and Rita are taking him seriously now.

The weight I've lost I won't gain back on rice. After lunch, I lie down on a bamboo mat and nap as I did in earliest childhood. The first heat of summer no longer bothers me. The sun is a furnace in Xi'an but the air is a fine screen and when I wake I can feel the faint winds coming in from the high plateau.

After dinner, everything begins to change. We have been invited to a party at the Foreign Language Institute. It is time to set out. I hike up to the fifth floor and knock on Wacker's door. It takes him a minute to answer. He is bleeding from his elbow to his shoulder. Just a bicycle accident, he says.

It takes him twenty minutes to get ready. Inertia has settled over Rick Wacker like an iron coat. He slips into black cotton shoes, the local kind, flat with no arch. His feet are huge, probably the biggest in Xi'an. He wraps his arm in a torn undershirt. "Why don't you tell me what happened?" I say.

Wacker gave Dr. Hou's wife a ride to the Xiaozhai market this morning. A traffic cop spotted them riding in tandem, chased them, caught them, and kicked out the back tire when they wouldn't stop. "We fell down in the fucking street," Wacker bellows. "The cop kept screaming. Not at me, of course. At her."

"Everybody rides two to a bike," I point out.

Wacker doesn't know what the problem is; perhaps a new round to combat Spiritual Pollution—that is, association with things Western. Dr. Hou's wife has been ordered to write an official self-criticism. So has Wacker.

When we finally set out together along the high brick wall of the campus, which runs south a half-mile into the suburbs, I can't keep up with Wacker. He rides in a furor, without looking back. The women sweep the gutters, and the dust rises up and resettles in the broom's wake like the vapors of a dismembered apparition.

I turn east onto the dirt trail that snakes through a village of mud houses—the old shortcut to the Foreign Language Institute. A few children always come out to watch me ride through. I can see that Wacker has already reached the highway. I back off on the pedals to a glide. At the entrance to the Institute, mosquitoes stream out of a cabbage field damp with the manure of man and pig, into the black belly of the sky.

When I arrive, the foreign students and teachers are dancing in the shadows of the courtyard. Someone from the Institute has wired in four-pole lamps and a portable stereo from the nearest dorm. I grope for beer in the zinc-lined cooler. It reminds me of the pop cooler at the gas station near the house where I was born. I open the long green bottle and siphon a deep gulp.

I feel as warm as the evening, the sweat like a light mist on my skin. I am thinking of how my former life and what I called a self has flaked off like dead skin. Afternoons when I ride into the city, through its seven mile wall, under the old archers' towers into the back streets of Xi'an, I can leave everything to chance. Engulfed by the Chinese, I do not want to be anywhere else in the world.

Two young Chinese students join the dancers. They are awkward, but enthusiastic. The two old Chinese women who sit together under one of the pole lamps, the official chaperones, remain expressionless.

At eleven, Wacker reminds me that the gates to the Medical College are closing. Wouldn't be the first time we had to wake the gatekeeper. We laugh. The lady chaperones have not risen once from their wooden folding chairs. The evening is still warm.

At midnight, one of the foreign teachers is prevented from leaving the Institute. The gates are locked and nobody will be allowed to go home. This is absurd, of course, because we all have to go home; we all have to work the next day. We gather together and set out by tacit agreement to make a show of force at the gate so they will open it and let us all out.

Hearing our plan, plenty of Chinese students pour out of the dorms and join our march. At the gatehouse porch, a group of gatekeepers entertain our protests and pleas, shaking their heads indifferently. The Chinese students who have followed us seem amused. "After all," one of them tells Wacker, "It's a rule. The gates must be closed at midnight."

We wait. The onlookers surround us until there is barely room to stand. Wacker tells me that the crowd is turning hostile. They are saying that we are troublemakers. Some are calling us foreign bastards. One is even saying we should be beaten up. That sentiment is palpable. The crowd presses into us, and I want to strike back. I feel their rage and then my own. A moment ago, there was nothing at this gate, no feeling, and now there is a violence on both sides, beyond reason.

Wacker pushes me forward toward the gate. Then he hands me his bike. He puts both hands on the rungs of the gate and scrambles quickly to the top. Astraddle the gate, he reaches back down. I lift his bike up by its rear tire. The crowd sees what we are doing and hisses; they surge forward. My ribs smack against the bars. Wacker has tossed his bike to the ground outside. I clear a space with my elbows and hoist my bike up. Wacker lifts it from my hands. I begin to climb, feeling nothing, my hands and knees tearing at the rungs. I want out. There's no other thought. Over the top, I float to the ground; the sky is starless and the gated courtyard glows in the blackness like the mouth of a kiln.

When we reach the Medical College, lights are out and this gate, too, is chained. Wacker can't rouse the keeper. A student passing on the other side helps us lift our bikes over. Wacker sits down in the stair well, slumping over like someone betrayed. Then he jumps up and goes upstairs.

In the light on my landing I see blood smeared on the front fender of my bike. I think: Wacker's reopened his wound. Inside, I discover that I have cut open my own fingertips on the gate.

I can't sleep. I switch on the shortwave, search the bands, but the only English voice is from North Korea. "Today our Glorious Leader visited the. . . ." I turn it off.

I don't bother to set the alarm. Every morning a violet haze pastes the sky to the earth, and I start coughing. The dust is caked like fine filings of rust in the lines of my palms. I always wake early in China now.

II. DUST

MASS IN LATIN

I've heard rumors of an active Catholic Church for weeks, but its existence remained no more substantial than a ghost until, at a dinner at the Xi'an Hotel last night, I overheard a man from Ireland say that he attends mass every Sunday. Wielding a full bottle of Tsing Tao beer, I entered into negotiations, and before the big green bottle was half-down, he agreed to meet me at mass this morning. "But you'll need full directions," he insisted, and he drew me a map in Gaelic.

After careful collation with my Chinese map, I set out early, arriving at a side street in the western sector where no foreigner has any reason to walk. Last night the man from Ireland warned me that the cathedral gate was entirely unremarkable, opening to the sidewalk like a thousand other gates in a thousand other walls. But every store and school, apartment and factory has its own gate and wall, I responded.

"This one is different," he insisted. "During the Cultural Revolution, they closed the cathedral down and built a candy factory around it."

Indeed, it turns out to be so. The cathedral is concealed within factory walls. I look around for my friend and check my watch: it has stopped. I risk entry, walking thirty paces into the compound. I meet a candy worker, but he doesn't challenge me. The walkway between low buildings ends in a cul-de-sac, an ascending ramp leads up to the right, and there, as though backed into this blind alley and left at a service entrance, is the cathedral—a two-story building of white stone in impeccable Romanesque style, as out of place here as the Cathedral of Notre Dame would be set down in a corner of Red Square.

The condition of the exterior is superb—no cracks, scars, or hammer marks. For some reason the Red Guard had spared its facade from the usual mutilations. A wide plaza undoubtedly extended to the street until 1973, when the new confectionery storerooms went up. In these pinched quarters the Cathedral of Xi'an resembles a monolithic relic shunted to the backlot of China's modernization program. No one has thought to dust it off as a showpiece for visiting diplomats and businessmen yet, either; it's strictly for the Chinese, who begin to arrive while I wait. Old men and women are whom I expected to see—those of long faith and endurance—but others I haven't expected—young peasants, couples, and families with a baby boy or girl hugging a hymnal. I crouch on a narrow band of asphalt until the man from Ireland arrives; we enter the church together, the only foreigners.

The interior of the cathedral is cool and stuffy, festooned

with a few icons from the West, its high ceiling wedged in place by a dozen lumbering columns painted red. There are two dozen rows of dark wooden pews. The ceiling tiles and upper moldings are of Oriental design, but almost invisible in the suspended darkness. A painting of St. Francis, a skull at his feet, peers sadly down. Simple stained-glass windows, a few panes missing, let in a bit of light, but everything possesses the shopworn glaze of wet ash. Paintings depicting the stations of the cross hang in gilded frames. Christ's humiliation has lost its remoteness here; his denunciation by the people in the streets of the city is a familiar scene, vivid as a postcard.

We choose a hard pew on the left. The raised sanctuary is obscured by one of the round columns. I crane my neck to view the altar. Two bare wooden confessionals abut the lip of the sanctuary, one at either end, each lacking a door or curtain to conceal the confessor. Those wishing to speak to a priest simply approach the open booths, turn their backs to the congregation, and speak through a wide opening. It is a rather public confessional and the lines are long. Even children wait a turn. When old women finish speaking to a priest, they remove their head scarves, swatches of white or black cloth, and hand them to others in line. No one takes much notice of us. It is one of the few places in Xi'an where a foreigner can stop moving and not draw a crowd.

The mass is one long rising and falling chant in Latin, more spoken than sung. The priest performs the ritual at the rear of the sanctuary, his back to us, his voice inaudible in the din and distance. In the pew to my right, the man leading the chant sinks down on his kneeler, consulting a little red book of Chinese characters he marks with his thumb. Enunciating the Latin syllable by syllable, his voice drones on like sticky syrup fed through a rolling mill. Beside him another man, fat and flushed by Xi'an standards, fingers a long rosary diligently.

The mass winds through its forty-year-old forms, and the priest comes down to administer communion. He is an imperial figure clad in crisp white muslin vestments and a crimson surplice of silk. As he blesses wafer and wine, he speaks to each worshipper. His voice trips with a stutter and halt; he makes the sounds of one who has suffered a premature stroke.

Afterwards I meet him outside. We are all standing under a banner, one end tied to the cathedral, exhorting the confectionery workers to greater profits. The cathedral was built a hundred years ago by Italian missionaries, the priest says. It is now the official Catholic Church of Xi'an, reopened in 1980. Of what he or the church suffered in the Cultural Revolution, he will not speak; he purses his lips and smiles. He says he had been elevated to the Bishopric of Xi'an. All his teeth are broken out.

Odd what survives: a dead language, a resurrected bishop. My friend tells me that the priests in China speak better Latin today than those in Italy. For a moment I can believe nothing has happened here, no one was beaten, nothing was smashed, but everything on the inside of the inner walls of this cathedral has its own litany of exodus, concealment, and return. In the recesses of these walls are blue tapestries embossed with red characters draped over tiered shrines of fresh flowers, and, above these displays, paintings of Madonna and Child on a background of solid gold set in a rounded frame, red as blood. Red, blue, and gold are the colors of the faith here, but one must look closely to see them in the dust and shadows of the interior.

The brick and stone are a blinding white in the noon sun. At the gate the Bishop says farewell. Across the street children without slippers run rings around the communal water pump. Their parents squat beside the earthen walls of their homes, clearing the coating of dust from their throats, stare our way, then stretch, waking from their naps, glad today is their free afternoon of the week. Everyone is eager for a stroll down West Big Street, for window shopping, for an ice lolly, and later for shish kebab and more shopping among the candles in the night market. It is a fine Catholic neighborhood, I suppose, but without a single Catholic.

My friend wonders what time it is. He is exhausted, perhaps from the heat. We end up in the Bell Flower Hotel after a long walk to the center of the city. Thirsty, we barge through the lobby into the restaurant and bark to a small dining room, where because of the in-between hour we are seated but not fed. I settle for beer in a can. We listen to the chug of the air-conditioner in the wall. It might be installed backwards for all the good it does. The hotel is new, modern, monstrous. The rats moved in the day it opened, they say. My friend starts talking about a priest he knows in the north of China, but I am thinking of the two photographers, one seated in a rear pew, the other standing outside the cathedral, who have surreptitiously snapped our portraits. I think of how few Xi'an Chinese own such fine cameras. "Those two photographers," I start to say, then stop. "Yes, I know," my friend says. "Did you think they were Japanese tourists?"

I finish my beer. The man from Ireland isn't drinking on Sunday. I'm sure he was once a priest, but I don't ask. When the waitress comes, we explain that we work in Xi'an, meaning we will pay in Chinese money, not in foreign exchange. She will have to do the paperwork. Much later she returns with our workers' cards. As we walk out, I notice a cook wringing out laundry in the water fountain. He is singing. Outside, in the strong afternoon light, the blue bricks and red columns of the Bell Tower are bleached white; and under the crazed tiles of its golden dome, caravans of traffic circle: the tires of bicycles and buses, the hooves of beasts of burden, the soles of the shoes of the haulers clacking loosely across the hot expanse of pavement.

THE TWO GIRLS AT THE AIRPLANE INSTITUTE

The People's Republic of China is about as titillating as a Nancy Drew detective novel, and Rick Wacker seems to have adapted to this general sexlessness as thoroughly as to soft cotton shoes. What he needs is some derring-do, says Rita, and with her help, I maneuver Wacker into accepting a dinner invitation at the apartment of the two girls at the Airplane Institute, provided I tag along as chaperone.

The two girls at the Airplane Institute came straight out of Swarthmore into Xi'an with great big red stars in their eyes and promptly alienated nearly every other foreign teacher in the city, but by the time I met them, they had settled into a fashionable cynicism. For some reason, no one much cared for them anyway, perhaps because they were so damned young or because, as everyone found out eventually, they had thrown themselves—without encouragement—at two guys from Stanford who were on a two-year volunteer teaching stint at Xi'an Polytechnic. I can't for the life of me understand why they failed in this seduction; perhaps they were too bold, too deliberate, or too doctrinaire. At any rate, Brunhilda, the tall blonde, and Mouse, the short brunette with dog-tired eyes and not much to say, are in love with Wacker, and he not only ignores them, he flees from them.

It has rained on and off without much restraint this morning, the day of Rick Wacker's big date, and when I finally trudge up the five flights to fetch him, he refuses to budge. "Tell them I'm sick," he pleads. "I think I really am." I tell him I've never been more disgusted by a single human being in my life. "You mean you don't want to go either?" he asks. "I certainly don't blame you," he adds.

So out of courtesy I find myself biking alone to dinner along the southern edge of the city wall, eastward, unsure where the Institute is, but determined to prove that at least one poor lad among us retains a sense of honor. Eventually I discover a promising gateway. Like a hundred other campuses in the vicinity, the Airplane Institute is new, its architecture the worst one could do with three- and five-story blocks of cement. The rain has returned by now, too. I am completely drenched. In crudest Chinese, I indicate to passersby that I need to find the apartment of the two foreign teachers. I am directed by successive informants ever deeper into the compound and finally deposited at the mouth of a vast dormitory. There Brunhilda spots me and comes right down. When I give her the news about Wacker's stomach flu, she's silent.

I am formally received on Floor Four by their official chaperone and made to log in. After negotiations, I am ushered into the girls' sealed-off quarters. Our dinner stew is boiling away on a single electric burner on the floor—potatoes and a lot of other all too familiar vegetables, and some sort of mystery gravy. We eat in the living room. It is the most dismal of their dismal rooms: a sofa covered in scratchy woolen blankets, blackout curtains on the windows—the kind of room where you could imagine nervously waiting out a Japanese bombing raid. Windows, unlike gates and walls, aren't a particular necessity of Chinese life.

Between bites Mouse shows me some of the treasures that visiting businessmen have flung their way, the chief goody being a bottle of Johnny Walker Red, now nearly empty. The girls seem to know quite a few sugar daddies of that ilk and aren't shy about being sharks; but few of us in Xi'an are any less opportunistic. Brunhilda and Mouse, moreover, are paid slave's wages, hardly a hundred kwai a month. The capper is that they are watched over by a host of Chinese scorpions, the sort of riffraff that often seems to wash up in Foreign Affairs Offices, those who can't speak foreign languages and hate foreigners, but have good connections and can use the excuse of hosting foreigners to procure all sorts of imported luxuries. In the meantime, if the foreigners themselves get too uppity, you can always force them to write self-criticisms, which Brunhilda and Mouse have done for certain infractions—tardiness, mostly.

I feel bad about the girls' situation at the Airline Institute, but they've not only come to accept it, they are negotiating to teach a second year which amazes me. When we finish the stew, we go straight to the bottle. Brunhilda and Mouse polish off most of it, then curl up together on the couch as though they are about to smooch. A delegation of Chinese students marches in, unannounced, and say they are ready to accompany us to the movies.

The campus auditorium is showing Hitchcock's *Rebecca*. They have, as usual, a full house, and the film is in its second or third reel by the time we wedge into a seat. I've never seen the picture, it is dubbed into Chinese, and makes not the slightest bit of sense, especially when the students, who know the plot by heart, begin explaining it in scrambled English. I try to stay alert by imagining how the Chinese imagine our life in the West, a projection of the old movies they've seen, no doubt: dark drawing rooms in which life is an unending routine of lies and deceits. Their impression is approximately correct.

After the movie Brunhilda and Mouse say they'll meet me later at the Xi'an Hotel which we foreigners call the Binguan, meaning Guesthouse. I ride alone to the hotel. It is still raining, exactly as it would in a bad soap opera. The Sudanese students are camped out in the second floor bar. When Brunhilda and Mouse arrive, they go off with Raoul. Every night Raoul tries to spike my beer with cheap vodka. By the time the trio returns, Brunhilda is sporting Raoul's watch and telling everyone she is engaged—a good thing, too, because Rick Wacker just walked in the door and is feeling no pain.

By closing we are all tipsy. The buses have stopped running, so Wacker and I gallantly offer the rear fenders of our bikes as a means to whisk Brunhilda and Mouse back to the Airplane Institute (which has thoughtfully forbidden the girls to ride bikes). Bikes are dangerous, especially when the driver can't see straight. With Mouse on the back, I feel as if I am pedaling uphill. When Wacker reaches the gates of the institute, for some reason he just falls over, and I'm so close on him I smash into Brunhilda and end up scraping both my knees on the street. The girls disappear, as unaffected as ever, beyond the gate.

Wacker is on a laughing jag and can't quit. He helps me straighten my handle bars, then insists on leading me home via a shortcut through the suburbs. I am dubious, particularly when he sets out at his usual Tour de France clip. I keep falling further behind. My knees are bleeding through my jeans, and the portion of my head which thinks is bricked up. The streets are dark and I quickly lose sight of Wacker. The suburbs lengthen into country roads, like some distended landfill of Silly Putty.

It is silent, save for a lonesome oncoming truck or jeep. To keep following this road, not knowing when or where Rick Wacker will turn off, is a form of madness; still, I keep hoping I'll find him at the next intersection or the next, waiting for me. After all, he has to turn west somewhere. I ride on. But of course he might have already turned off. Somewhere back there perhaps. How would I ever know, that son of a bitch? He's not one to wait.

Ahead, the darkness is completely filled in with black — with black *what*, I don't know, but it is bigger than any sky I've ever seen. The road has no center line and no particular reason for being, because it does not seem to lead to anything — no communes, no mud houses. I expect the macadam to run out soon, to turn into packed clay, to be overgrown, to peter out into a Spirit Way and end in the cellar of some tumulus, a royal house of bone and vinegar jars. South of Xi'an, the jaws were opening wide to swallow up the dimension of size itself and perspective, too, along with time and gravity and electromagnetism, reducing them all to the real base elements—wind and dust. Oblivion, that is. I begin to sing at the top of my lungs. There is nothing left to do, finally, but ride back the long way I've come, hoping I won't be flattened somewhere along the way by a night truck traveling with its headlights out.

The night is busy sucking me in piece by piece—nostrils, eyelashes, beard, lips, eyeballs and orbital sockets, finger-nails and teeth and root canals, popping off the skin like a fine glove, draining all the blood through my kneecaps until there is nothing but skeleton, bones pedaling a black bike frame without tires or tubes across fields of rapeseed and armchair graves . . . assisting in my own devouring, sucked dry as a seed husk, riding on until eternity or a rampaging PLA troop truck smacks into me head-on—an engorged caribou, bellowing in heat; a night as big as Hudson's Bay. . . .

DR. FU SMELLS THE BLOOD OF AN ENGLISHWOMAN

Fred and Rita are due out of Xi'an at noon for a month's vacation, but their permits to Tibet haven't come through yet.

I'll miss them if they go. Their bathtub heaterbox burnt out a week ago and they've been taking showers at my place. Rita prefers a shower in the morning, Fred in the afternoon. I always have the hot water waiting for them, seventeen minutes from fill to full delivery temperature. Usually we sit down for a while first anyway in my two living room chairs like Deng Xiaoping and a visiting head of state, minus our delegations—minus, for that matter, the spittoons at our feet. Both Fred and Rita like talking about Japan, about Japanese onsens, the food, the big money paid by businessmen for private language lessons; about the ninety-minute commute into Tokyo, too, but also about the cleanliness. For Fred and Rita, these are scenes from a previous life. For me, it's like being in the presence of mediums who, from within the heart of this faceless campus of cement (located somewhere between two T'ang pagodas), can call up the cheery details of a land of luxury, of beauty, of Oriental grace otherwise absent from this Oriental continent.

What I like best about Rita in particular is her refusal to put up with Chinese bullshit, which is exactly like bullshit in the West, only more bureaucratic. She doesn't ignore it or step around it; she confronts it and asks whose job it is to clean it up. When she and Fred took a New Year's trip west to Urumqi, they were told that their hotel room there was five kwai a night but Rita had heard from earlier travelers that the price was three kwai. The storm in the lobby that night was such that travelers long afterward reported that Rita was still being talked about—the banshee with the backpack, a legend of the new Silk Road. Her sutras are summons to simple efficiency. Every third week, as I've mentioned, she naturally suffers a complete collapse, they wheel out the oxygen tank and in a few days she's back, ready to beat the shit out of the lackeys in hotels and restaurants and stores and train stations who try to charge us too much or claim they don't have what we want. She takes on cadres, Confucians, and all the other masters of foot dragging, past and present. Fred, on the other hand, has spent twenty years on the low roads of Asia and the Mideast, and it is his view that at ground level it's best to expect nothing.

It didn't surprise me that Rita and Fred were issued their month's pay, including travel bonuses, in one-kwai notes. Two thousand of them. Rita sat down and counted every last one of them; Fred carried the loot home in a shoe box—just the sort of thing you want to carry across China to Tibet on buses and second-class trains. Rita stayed long enough to tell off the entire Foreign Affairs Office.

They would never have gotten out of Xi'an today had it not been for Dr. Fu. Wacker and I have been helping them pack for a week, rifling through everything they were going to discard for what we might need in their absence—foodstuffs, mostly. Professor Zhong has repeatedly intervened with the sluggish Foreign Affairs Office to procure the special travel permits Fred and Rita need for Lhasa. Everyone said everything was in order. All of us must have told Rita a hundred times to relax. Then this morning the word came that they couldn't leave because Tibet had never received a copy of their passports. At that point even Professor Zhong found the situation hopeless. Instead of flying into a rage, Rita broke down and cried.

None of us could blame her. When she started crying on the landing, Dr. Fu came out and took over. He forced the crew who ran the only copy machine on campus to open up early; he made copies of Fred and Rita's passport; he had them posted for Lhasa by noon. Then he drew them aside and said, "Go west. By the time you reach the border, they'll be expecting you. All I have to do now is call ahead and assure them that your documents are in good order and on the way. If you still get the runaround, show them this letter. It's one of the best I've ever written."

Documents in order, Rita and Fred, Wacker and I, all pile into a campus limousine, fetched after much finagling by Professor Zhong. We reach the Xi'an train station in time; the train is standing at the platform. They hesitate a second as they step up into their car, looking our way, back at Xi'an. Their train leaves exactly on time. It is a steam locomotive, a real screamer, the overnighter to Chengdu. Gone for a month. That doesn't seem possible, as close as we've been for so long—although it isn't long.

Wacker and I spread out in the back seat like millionaires, speeding south, horn at full blast, dividing up the spoils Fred and Rita left us. Of course, we're part of what they left behind, too, and we'll probably wake up tonight, disturbed by some new quietness, reduced by half.

— : : —

With Fred and Rita gone, Rick Wacker and I begin to rot away in the rooftop disco now open at the Binguan. We scour Xi'an's small shops for odd lots of Tsing Tao beer and shelled almonds in a can; failing that, we walk the fourteen flights to the roof, stopping at each warden's desk to ask if they'll sell us beer from the floor's stock in the fridge. If we arrive empty handed, we have to start over in the lobby by signing a special chit which entitles us to spend an exorbitant set amount of Chinese money for the drinks above, which otherwise require hard currency.

Most of the time we stay out too late to retrieve our bikes from the hotel parking shed. The keeper closes up at about eleven. If we can't wake him, we have to walk the two miles home, and Wacker always sets a killing pace.

Tonight an American tour group happens to have commandeered most of the second floor lounge. They're from Indianapolis. They've decided to costume themselves for the occasion. One strapping cowboy is dressed down to a diaper and a torn T-shirt; he carries a flashlight and calls himself the Statue of Liberty, although he looks like a hefty Baby New Year. The young ladies wear exceedingly brief costumes, too. It is Mardi Gras in Xi'an, and Rick Wacker and I, along with a dozen bewildered Chinese, station ourselves along one side of a table to take in the orgy. The tourists end up buying us drinks and, when they hear about our pitiful lives here, shower us with pilfered room soap. The Chinese contemplate this orgy in silence, trying to understand another culture, I suppose. It's impossible.

The next morning, a bit hung over, I answer the pounding at the door and find one of my students on the landing. He has just met an American doctor, an ophthalmologist who apparently cornered me last night and requested a tour of the campus hospital. Somehow she's managed to take the bus and reach my doorstep, all without a word of Chinese. I'm astounded. With my faithful student at my side, we arrange a hospital visit.

I've never been in the wards myself, never closer than to get a look at the patients wandering around outside in their pajamas. Inside, matters are no less informal. The patient rooms resemble student dorms: four or five beds in a row, a thermos on every dresser. Family members frequently spend the night on cots, awaiting word when treatment will begin. We are allowed to talk with a boy whose eye has been poked out. We visit a lab. We are told about various methods of treating the eye.

Afterwards, when the American ophthalmologist comes up to use my bathroom, she says things in the Xi'an hospital seemed roughly thirty years behind—not bad, she thinks. We put her back on the bus. I elevate my student, Mr. Jing Lin-Huang, to the position of Supreme Middleman in light of his services. He's lousy in English class, but on the outside he's superb at getting things done. Once, on a bet, he'd even been able to talk his way into the Friendship Store forbidden to Chinese citizens.

Jing seems far more worldly than the other students, who have only the vaguest notions of an outside world, of America in particular. When I tell him how much an ophthalmologist earns in America and describe a doctor's life down to the minutest detail—the station wagon and the BMW, the garage with remote-control door opener, the lawn mower, the three personal telephones, the separate bedrooms for each child and one for the dog, the gas barbecue on the patio, and the exact dimensions of each patio brick, its cost, and where you could buy it on a Saturday afternoon—he thinks I am a wonderful teller of tales.

When I get back to my apartment, Dr. Fu is waiting on the landing. He wants to borrow back his bike. For a moment I can't remember where it is. Unhappily, it did not accompany me home from the Binguan last night.

The problem is that an American has expired aboard a tour bus on the way back from the vaults of the Emperor Qin, and Dr. Fu has been summoned to the central morgue of Xi'an. The deceased was a retired gynecologist on holiday—seven cities in seventeen days with deluxe accommodations. She keeled over in her seat from a massive coronary at age sixty-seven. Beyond dropping her off downtown on the way to the hotel, no one knows what to do.

Dr. Fu and I take the bus downtown. I'm just to tell them I'm a visiting medical student. We're met by three nervous senior physicians and the chief cadre of China International Travel Service. The corpse has been stripped and placed on a gurney, awaiting its turn at an autopsy. A team of medical students gather round, clutching thermos lids, inspecting the flabby pink remains. I have never seen a dead body before, nor a sixty-seven-year-old woman naked, for that matter. My head is a little light. I weave toward a table by windows so caked up with coal dust I can't see out.

Meanwhile Dr. Fu requests a death certificate. I help him fill it out in English. Then he tries to place a call to the American Embassy in Beijing but is never connected. The body of Mrs. Meriwether, we're told, cannot be examined or shipped home until authorization is received from Beijing. "They mean before enough FEC is sent to pay them," Dr. Fu whispers. After filling out several more forms in Chinese, he leaves the the morgue, which begins to look as gruesome as a warehouse of animal body parts to be used for making traditional medicines.

On our way home, Dr. Fu purchases a twenty-kilo sack of rice, which he dumps on the landing we share. Of his colleagues downtown, he says they could have stood there staring at the corpse for a week, waiting to be paid. They wouldn't even put her on ice until Dr. Fu authorized foreign funds from the Medical College.

"Can you do that?" I ask.

"No," he says. "But I did it anyway. A little thing like ice can be important. I mean, what do they think we're going to ship home? After a while you don't even have a corpse. Have you ever smelled blood when it begins to go bad?"

It is clear that Dr. Fu has, and too often.

He shakes his head, walks inside, and cranks up his Beethoven tape. I don't ask him anymore about the suicide pact; it's too painful.

TAXI

The Xi'an Hotel is a rare point of contact with English-speaking foreign tourists whom we can cajole into exchanging money. I've spent many a cool spring evening sitting in its main lobby, watching groups from America and Europe enter the two elevators, their luggage piled about for later delivery to their rooms. Perhaps I was looking for a familiar face; if so, I never saw one.

The hotel honors our white worker's cards so that we can spend our worthless local currency on decent food and beer and, now, in the summer, its open air rooftop disco for foreign tourists is the best place to kill time. Rick Wacker and I have been doing too much of that together lately. If there are no tour groups in town, we're often almost alone on the roof. At dusk, the pigeons swoop down from the Little Wild Goose Pagoda next door; when it's dark, the rats run freely across the empty dance floor.

On one such dead evening, Wacker tells me the story of Wen De. It surprises me, given his seeming reluctance to become involved with expatriate women. He met Wen De a year ago, when she still worked in the Binguan. One floor up from the lobby is a restaurant, lounge, and hall of poorly-lighted counters stuffed with high-priced treasures — laquerwork, cloisonne vases, postcards, picture books, rubbings. Each section is presided over by a young woman in a starched white blouse, black skirt, patched and sagging nylons, and black high heels. They all look unashamedly bored. One evening Wacker was strolling by and heard a clerk minding the counter by herself murmur in low, low English a plea so monotonic it begged for a reply. It sounded as if she were saying, "Please help me."

Wacker stopped. He asked if she had said something. "Oh nothing," she answered. Her voice was deep and playful. She was reading an English-language textbook. Wacker told her that he taught English at the Medical College. She wanted to know how long he would be in China. Then she asked him to help her with her homework.

Help meant that Wacker should fill in all the answers. She handed him a pencil. He filled in the blanks rapidly. She barely nodded when he handed it back. She was not a great beauty: plain, solid, rounded everywhere, without edge or crease, and tall for a Chinese woman. She wrote down her name: Wen De Mai. When Wacker turned to walk away, she said, "If you want a cab, come to the gate at ten."

Wacker didn't find a taxi cab at the Binguan gate at ten, but Wen De met him there and they walked north in the dark. It was impossible to tell what she had in mind. A block away they came to a taxi, the first one Wacker remembered seeing in Xi'an. It was a Russian Bear, a sort of Mercedes clone which had been through the ringer, drained of color and dented, but inside, it was soft, leather cushioned. The driver was so short Wacker could see only the back of his blue baseball cap. They tore off at a high speed without lights. Wacker had no idea what would happen then.

Few shopgirls in China could afford a taxi, let alone an all-night taxi, but the meter in this cab was not running. Wen De asked Wacker to teach her to swear in English. Before long they were conspiring to write an English-language textbook modeled after *Follow Me,* the most popular one in China; they were calling their version *Follow Me, Shithead.* Then Wen De told Wacker that she was so bored all the time, she hated to stand behind the counter and talk to the old ladies from America—it was all such a big (what do you call it?) piss-off. But she had no choice. The job was assigned. She called it her punishment—punishment for what, she wouldn't say. At times Wen De engaged in long, disagreeable exchanges with the driver. Finally, she told Wacker he had to get out. The street was an unfamiliar one, but Wen De was adamant. "You get out here," she repeated, with a flick of her hand.

Wacker opened the door and stood in the street. Wen De rolled down the window and pointed him home. She laughed. Her eyes were pure black. The streets were the same everywhere, one thing looked like another, the walls went everywhere, around every corner.

It was a curious encounter, I agreed.

Wacker swore to avoid her after that. He felt there would

be trouble. She was one of the disaffected for whom China is the Big Bang gone bust. They're part of a generation promised the moon, says Wacker, but all that's been delivered are truckloads of meteorites the size of dumplings. They'll do almost anything—if not to get out, then just to do something not permitted.

Wacker kept his distance until last May Day. Classes were cancelled and he was summoned to join the delegation from the Medical College to Qing Xing Park. Qing Xing is where at the turn of the century the Empress Dowager, fleeing the Forbidden City, moored her court in exile after failing to scare the West. The May Day banquet was a chance to fete as many foreign workers as possible at once; time, too, for their hosts to fatten themselves at another official trough. Wacker managed to slip away from Professor Zhong quickly enough. He wanted to see what the locals were doing to amuse themselves. Most of them were shoving their way toward a temple on the lakeshore. The temple was erected on a twelve foot high pedestal; beneath it, acrobats were warming up to perform. Wacker wormed his way up the stairs, but found the temple as hopelessly clogged as a city bus. The acrobats were somewhere below; he couldn't quite separate them from the crowds. In one lower courtyard, however, he spotted Wen De, and unable to go against the surge back down the temple stairs, Wacker lowered himself over the side. As he dropped, he felt hands grabbing his feet, his knees, his crotch, his arms; he was set down a few feet from Wen De, who shook her finger at him and then said to meet her by the boats at dark.

For the May Day banquet in the main pavilion, the Friendship Committee provided bottles of sweet pop, Xi'an Beer, a dozen uniformally uninspired but generous dishes, speakers and dancers, and foreign teachers roped into delivering speeches and songs. At dusk Wacker left his seat to go to the bathroom and kept walking. He saw a few families still on the lake, flailing with heavy oars. Then Wen De appeared. They walked along one path, then another. She was all business. She described how after the foreigners went in for their banquet the police broke up the performance of the acrobats, beat the crowds back with sticks, and hauled off two of her friends. She said it had all happened before, many times.

They emerged in a parking lot of army jeeps, vans, and limousines with red flags — the back lot for cadres only. Wen De said they had to wait there for her uncle. He would come only when it was completely dark. Then the taxi they had taken from the Binguan pulled into the lot. Wen De spoke to the driver, her uncle. He wore the same blue baseball cap as before. They got in and drove out of the park. Wen De said her uncle had been on the Long March; later he worked in the Fourth Military Hospital; now he drove a taxi through Xi'an all night.

"Why all night," Wacker asked.

"Because he can't stand to see Xi'an by day," Wen De answered, laughing.

He asked what would happen to her two friends.

She didn't know. It was always something different. Jail for a while or work camp or nothing. She said her friends were all bad. They would laugh at pictures of Chairman Mao, listen to Voice of America broadcasts, attend parties, play Hong Kong disco music. At night they would accost foreigners coming out of the Binguan, talk English, ask for ballpoint pens, exchange money. She remembered one summer when a teacher from America took some of them with him to the rooftop disco. There was a big fight—no Chinese are allowed. But the American teacher was a gangster; they all stayed and danced. Later, they were punished. Her father told her that she was no longer his daughter.

"Was your father an important man?" Wacker wondered.

"He worked for Public Security."

"So," Wacker said, "he got you a job in the hotel."

"That was true," she said, "but it was no fun. It was no fun last year and no fun now."

The taxi entered through the archway tunnel in the eastern wall of the city, crossed town, and left by the western gate. Wen De stared listlessly at the candles on noodle stands, the night markets. The suburbs extended for miles; there was nothing to see. Wen De asked Wacker if he wanted to keep going. Yes, he did. She and her uncle drove this way all the time, not stopping until dawn.

"So you drove all night," I asked.

"All night," Wacker replied.

Sometime later, Wen De took him to what she called a "rock party," a get-together at an out-of-town cadre's house. In a room at the back was a tape player and a faulty strobe light; stuffed chairs were drawn into a circle; couples waltzed to Western music. They drank sweet coffee and sweet wine. Everyone agreed that anyone over thirty was either scared shitless or corrupt. Everyone wanted to go to America. If China could "change, man," then they'd come back, of course. But China could not change. China could never be free.

One night when Wen De and Wacker were riding through the streets, they all started laughing for no reason, even Wen De's uncle. It was near dawn. The cab stopped in the middle of the street. They'd run out of gas. They got out. They all walked off in different directions to their homes. It was summer, the sun was burning a hole in the well of dust, and the streets caught fire, the flames unrolling at the edges like pages of a burning book.

"You'd been up too long," I said.

"I needed to sleep," Wacker admitted, "but when I dreamed, it was as if I were still awake. In my dream I pushed my bike all the way to the Binguan and stuffed it in the back of Uncle's taxi; and the taxi was completely empty inside— no seats, no shift, not even a steering wheel."

"What finally happened?" I asked.

"She disappeared," he said.

One day last fall, at noon, Wacker discovered her uncle napping in his taxi across from the Binguan. Wacker tapped on the window. Uncle calmly flipped his sunglasses up on his forehead, just under the bill of his baseball cap, and motioned Wacker into the back. He hit the horn a solid blast and pulled across the oncoming traffic, driving all the way to the city wall.

Professor Zhong was standing at the curb. He wore his double-breasted pinstripe suit and red plaid tie. Opening the door without looking up, he murmured a greeting and slid in beside Wacker. The cab turned around, heading south across the moat. Professor Zhong studied the papers in his lap, cleared his throat, and said that Miss Wen was a fortunate young woman; her father had pulled some strings; she was now enrolled in the Polytechnic University at Changsha.

"So he shipped her off," I said.

"Not quite," said Wacker.

He hadn't believed Professor Zhong. At the gate to the Medical College, Professor Zhong stepped out, but Wacker kept riding. Uncle kept driving.

"Where is she?" Wacker asked.

Changsha. Wen De's father, Uncle explained, was a Big Man. By his order, for example, Uncle was permitted to drive his taxi where he wanted, when he wanted, answering to no one.

"Then take me to Wen De," Wacker said.

"That's impossible," Uncle answered.

"Give us a chance," Wacker said. "I won't leave Xi'an until she tells me to go."

"You can't stay here forever," Uncle pointed out.

They parked at the Binguan. It was raining. They stood side by side on the sidewalk. Uncle was very short. His left leg was stiff; it seemed to be welded straight, so it could never really bend—a legacy of the Long March, perhaps, or some more recent horror. Uncle pulled the sunglasses down over his eyes, solid black like a visor.

"Just tell me where she is," Wacker begged.

Uncle shook his head. "She's nowhere," he said. "She's a ghost now."

"So you don't know where she is," I said.

"Oh, but I do," says Wacker, "I do. I've seen her. She's being rehabilitated. She's with Emperor Qin and the terra-

cotta warriors. At the back of the pits with the other con-
scripts reassembling clay limbs. You can't get close, of
course. I doubt she's seen me in the crowds. But I've seen her.
Several times. At least I think it's her. From a distance. And
it's been so long. But I think it must be her. It happens all the
time this way."

III. RUINS

CHURCH
MUSIC

The MacLarens live in the downtown Renmin Hotel, the city's largest, ugliest, and most menacing inn. They are both scientists, or rather they were before they left Scotland; now they are teachers of English to scientists in Xi'an. When I told Ivan MacLaren about attending a Catholic mass, he said he knew where there was a Protestant church as well. Why not pay it a visit this Sunday? Sylvia would probably be keen for the adventure, too.

I'm keen first of all for my Sunday bath, which courtesy of Ivan and Sylvia is a nice change from my gutless shower. They are the only foreigners I know with a tub and hot water from the tap. I regularly drop in for a bath, then a beer. This Sunday is a bit different: bath, beer, and then off to church. None of us are in the least religious—we're like the average Chinese—but we're curious about how such an entirely Western form is handled here.

The Protestant church of Xi'an was not leveled during Mao's final push for the pure egalitarian state; rather, it was converted to serve new gods. When the Red Guards closed it down, they tore crosses from the rooftops and pasted anti-Christian posters across its outside walls. The church facade became an antireligious instruction mural. Then it was converted into offices. Now it's surrounded by still more offices, a wall, and a gate, but since 1980 it has again become a church—the official, government-organized Three-Self Church of Xi'an. It is a block from the Friendship Store where we foreigners can shop for the best imports and exports of China. No ordinary Chinese allowed.

It is easy enough to find. Although it is on a side street, deep inside an unmarked wall and gate, smothered by offices, it is made visible even from the sidewalk by a curious tower, part Oriental, part Northern European in design. It is said that the Three-Self Church has lured back only one in ten of the underground Christians, but even the courtyard is filled today. And inside, there are 500 worshippers.

The service is Protestant, recognizable and unremarkable, yet in every particular a few degrees from plumb. The church interior is without a picture of Jesus or Mary, without a tableau from the New Testament, without a single stained-glass window pane. The walls are adorned with a few hand-written scrolls. There are no crosses, save a crucifix of gold foil hung on the brick arch in the wall behind the pulpit. The collection box is on a pedestal posted in front, permitting everyone to see who gives and how much.

A bell sounds, bringing the first of three preachers to the lectern. He carries a glass of boiled water. On his right is a choir of twenty-seven women and three men, all dressed in unpressed white smocks. The choir closely resembles a team of lab technicians. The choirmaster's coat is too short in the arms and too high in the waist, but he shakes and flutters with overflowing panache. A woman in the pew in front of us presses a hymnal into my hands. I have no idea what page to turn to or how to read Chinese hymns, but the melodies are familiar enough, from "Holy, Holy, Holy" to "What a Friend We Have in Jesus." When I join in, Sylvia jumps up and leaves.

The hymns are accompanied by the worst piano in the world, an ordinary-looking contraption built in an extraordinary manner so as to play out of tune and only out of tune, a tune unto itself. I feel myself transported beyond mere flats and sharps into the pure realm of clang and clong—the Chinese Christian version of rapture.

Buttoned into a tight black robe, the first preacher begins his battle to deliver the longest sermon of the day. He speaks for one hour and fifteen minutes, pausing only to glance at the clear glass of water on the lectern which he never deigns to put to his lips. In the growing heat I watch that glass, delivering my own soliloquy on thirst, on the weakness of the flesh, on the tedium of oratory, whether political, religious, or scholastic. Fortunately, a boring speech proves no more intolerable in a foreign language than in one's own. I drift, waking only at the accession of a second preacher, then a third, who is probably a party member, a Three-Self cadre—when he delivers announcements and smiles, no one smiles back. There follows the Lord's Prayer, which should sound about the same whether in English or

Chinese, but the congregation recites it pell-mell. The service ends in disarray.

An usher removes the collection box and carries it into a room behind the pulpit. We can see into the back room. Two pastors and the Party man remove their robes and, under a picture of Jesus, count the money.

Someone at the gate approaches Ivan and writes out the address of a second Protestant Church, set to reopen next Sunday. Apparently it has been closed since the Cultural Revolution. Ivan insists that we track it down, but Sylvia demands we eat first. We ride a few blocks south to the Sian Restaurant for Health and Food Curing, a workers' restaurant where ordering is impossible but the food has been proven safe. Stained and moist, the oilcloth table covers there are considered elegant, as is beer served in a smudgy glass. We make it clear we want to spend a kwai and a half a piece. That yields four plates and soup with rice.

After lunch we set forth to find the second church. We have to ride out of Xi'an proper. A few blocks east of the moat, Ivan asks directions; we turn south and end up in a blind alley. Then my front tire goes flat. I roll up to the first bicycle shop we see and borrow the hand pump, but my tire will hold no air. It's a fine bike otherwise, a 1968 Phoenix without kickstand. The repairman invites me into his shop for consultation. The front wall of his establishment opens to the street; word of my arrival brings out the curious. I accept a six-inch-high stool and sit down in the midst of bicycle tools and parts. The floor is packed dirt. Two men and a boy work in their undershirts. One removes the tube. I know the tube well; it has been out three times in my presence, and a

hundred times before that, so it now resembles a sock of a
thousand patches. There is never any question today that it
will be patched in the same way again. Repairmen never
dream of throwing out a tube and starting over. Even a
foreigner with a flat would not be allowed to indulge in such
gross extravagance.

From the back of the shop a door opens and closes on an
inner residence. A little girl, three or four years old, advances
and retreats. Her father tells me that she is terrified; she takes
me for a Cossack. I stroke my beard. I tell her father I am *mei
guo ren,* American. That makes no impression whatsoever. It
would be better to be from Outer Mongolia. They keep me as
long as they can, the way one does when visitors drop in from
other planets, but they speak very little and I sit patiently on
my stool. We settle the bill at sixty fen. I find the MacLarens
outside. They've been directed to two more dead ends.

Here, east of the Xi'an gate, the place seems older and
poorer. Foreigners almost never stray here — no reason to do
so. We are almost treated like Chinese when we stop to order
yogurt, then ice cream. Sylvia hails a little boy on a bike and
hands him the paper on which is written the address we're
after.

"Follow me," he says in English, "I know Dong Guan."
We are skeptical.

He rides up three successively narrower, more crowded
side streets, first north, then west, then north again, moving
beyond the main streets and motorized traffic. The second of
these streets curves gently up a long rise, and the walls and
houses along its northern side are painted blue halfway up, at
about the height of a man; it's the only outdoor blue paint

I've seen in China. By its splattered texture, it appears that the paint was applied on the run, pitched from a can. Abruptly, the color blue ceases and gray resumes.

We turn north onto a brick path which jags and nose-dives a few blocks more. The boy stops at an iron gate. We thank him. It is the gate to a construction yard. Heavy equipment is parked at random within. There are sheds, warehouses, apartments, and, in the middle of the grounds, one plain, two-story church of whitewashed brick in the Northern European style. At the church entrance someone has parked a steamroller.

Dozens of pews are stacked inside the church and two men are painting a sort of wainscoting on the walls. They apply thick, hideous green paint like plaster. Near the front is a piano in its crate—a new piano, we are told. The church was built in 1931; it has been closed the past twenty years. A construction equipment company used the building, with its vaulted ceiling and solid walls, as a warehouse. It will continue to occupy the grounds. The church will indeed reopen in a week.

On our way back to the gate, we meet two old, old women in black, strolling hand in hand, and they tell us how they came to church here before the Cultural Revolution, before the revolution itself, in fact, and they remember us—yes, we are the Englishmen, aren't we. We say we are not quite English, but they don't believe us. They have last seen our faces in this very churchyard, the year I was born, before the steamrollers arrived, and they seem to fancy that we have returned at last, like birds of omen, on the eve of the reopening. This notion makes all the sense the world could ever make to the two sisters. It makes us possible, at least. They themselves, the most delicate of creatures, hand in hand, seem decidedly less possible for us, however—creations of Old China, of dynasties long dead. One sister leans on the other as she scrutinizes us matter-of-factly. Yes, we have come back after all, I can see her conclude. She has the tiniest bound feet I've ever seen.

— : : —

A week later, as the MacLarens and I are trying to retrace our steps to attend the reopening of the eastern Protestant Church, we can barely remember the way. We push on, however, finally skimming the blue wall. Where the paint stops we turn down the narrow brick path.

The steamroller has disappeared. The courtyard of gravel and sand is full of Chinese in pressed white shirts and blouses. It is a hot July day. Inside the church, the cheap, flat bamboo fans flutter like Ping-Pong paddles. Every pew is already full, and many more worshippers want to go inside, but as the only foreign guests we are the ones escorted through the side entrance to the front and, when the preacher pauses in his sermon, we are shown to a space made for us in the front pew. Perhaps we have returned from the dead.

Inside it is all the hotter, but the old preacher at the altar is not about to acknowledge it. He stokes his sermon with fierce gestures. I watch him from the front row as one does a figure on a movie screen, my neck craned. The audience is attentive. They know they are not at an opera, where everyone gaggles and gossips. They respect the specialist and listen. I am wondering how long he will continue speaking, but I am also wondering what this preacher has suffered. It doesn't show in his face, through his black-rimmed glasses. He looks quite average and happy, as though he has learned the true insignificance of everyone, himself included.

There are no paintings or stained glass in this second Protestant church either. The windows are those of an office or apartment, opening in. But there is fresh paint laid on like leather, garish lamps of green and red glass—the kind in America you can't buy even in K-Mart, but all the rage here, suspended from the rafters—vases of flowers on the pulpit and, under the vases, pleated white cloth. A grand opening. No crosses anywhere, not even a crucifix of foil, but the choir has new white robes. I recognize members of the choir. I saw them singing in the main church last week. They are splendid in their unstained gowns and for a moment this service becomes like any the world over, but then out of the corner of my eye I see the faces of those standing outside at the windows, looking in. They are looking in as people do in China, honestly and without shame, staring in as they sometimes do when we sit down in a restaurant and they spot us from the sidewalk. *Englishmen, maybe. Or Cossacks.*

The Three-Self Church has brought Christianity this much further into the open today where the government's hope is that it will die. Underground, in the home-churches, the faith is too intense, too threatened, to expire. There is at this moment at least one home-church leader in a jail in Xi'an for every month of the past two years. What am I attending? In what building am I dallying now? I rise in the midst of another sermon, walk through the back room, and step outside.

In the heavy equipment yard, I can see the people looking into the church, their backs to me now. Inside I looked in vain for the two old sisters in black. They aren't outside, either.

At the gate I come across a capitalist—an old man crouched over two open crates of Bibles. He has no vendor's license. He refuses to tell me where the Bibles are from, but he is selling them hand over fist and no one has come to stop him.

That night we splurge on dinner at the Renmin Hotel. From the window we can see the remains of the Han dynasty capital, broken walls of earth, tiles in a heap, the brush strokes of a pre-Christian city as great as ancient Rome, perhaps greater, never touched by the hint or breath of a Christian god—an image in the earth of China as it has been for most of its history, before the arrival of foreign gods at Xi'an.

Later, alone, I will think of the white the congregation wore this Sunday in July, when they were packed in like doves in the dark pews. White for communion, I realize at last, and two figures will pass before me like lashes blinking, hand in hand, white from head to foot, translucent as silk.

THE MAD
MONK OF
ZEN

China has swallowed me whole; there's nothing left, not so much as a toenail or a fingertip. All previous reference points have been erased. I've taken to rummaging through the ruins of Buddhist temples, strictly out of desperation, I think. Daily life is drab enough, there are piss-few resources of any kind. Fortunately, the MacLarens share in this pointless pursuit. We've spread out the maps on their bed in the Renmin Hotel and we think we know where the old temples were or at least where they stood before the Cultural Revolution, on sites over a thousand years old. Chest deep in this city of yellow dust, I'm looking to reinvent Chinese Buddhism at its source.

— : : —

No one remembers why the Big Wild Goose Pagoda — Dayanta — is so named. There's no formal record of its title. It has been the tallest structure in Xi'an since 652, when Xuanzhuang returned on foot from India with his backpack of sutras.

Early this morning, from the top of its seven harmonious stories, we have our first aerial view of Xi'an. Northward, the Ming dynasty walls enclose a low, modern city—a neat seven-mile rectangle etched in uniform boulevards and snaking back streets. Radiating outward are the patchy suburbs, universities, and factories, all the modern constructions of New China in a sprawl. The coalsack air and rising dust paint everything an amorphous gray. To the south, the royal burial mounds thrust upward from the plain; to the east, a hint of the sealed necropolis of China's first emperor is heaped like a tent of rich earth. The surrounding mountains and rivers are invisible in the haze.

Dayanta and its nearby companion, Xiaoyanta, the Little Wild Goose Pagoda, finished thirty-two years later, are the two great surviving monuments of China's golden T'ang dynasty. Nearly every other sign has been obliterated, but these two birds still tower over the fallen capital.

The Big Goose is the perfection in stone of an abstract notion: the horrifying simplicity of the infinite. Its body has long been gutted of Buddhist treasures. Kids descend into air-raid shelters beneath its courtyard and idle away the morning at old video games, cast off by Hong Kong merchants—an underground arcade with electronic mantras, a cool fire burning in the ashes.

— : : —

Daxingshan, near the Xiaozhai free market where I shop, is said to have been the greatest of all Chinese monasteries in its day. Since the third century, Daxingshan has been destroyed and rebuilt countless times, and the Red Guards did not spare it. They leapt on this venerable institution with tongs and hammer.

Daxingshan is a people's park now. Pay your admission, take a paper ticket, stroll the dull grounds. In the center there is a single small courtyard where once there were dozens. Extensive restorations are underway and the iron gate is usually locked, but today the gate is ajar. I don't hesitate.

Inside a superb reconstruction is underway, but it's so clean as to be fraudulent: carved steles white and swept, untouched even by the ink of rubbing masters; new roof tiles painted bright reds and golds. It's a dressing up of the ruins. Seventeen centuries later the meditation hall ends up selling souvenirs. I won't become a Buddhist in here.

Only outside, under the old gate, do I feel the old weight, where Daxingshan casts its shadow over the street. At noon, a line of school children passes by, followed by two of the dark peasant women of Shaanxi going to market in a hurry. I follow them, retracing my steps. In the market five Buddhist monks in brown robes swerve like frightened herons. The cabbage wagons wheel into line; vendors toss pork flanks at customers' feet, but the monks are as frail as paper—I can almost see through them.

— : : —

The summer clouds are empty; only the dust along the margins of streets and houses, turned to slime, reminds me of the recent brutality of mud and rain. I set out for Qing Long Si, the Green Dragon Temple, south of the city wall, following Sylvia MacLaren who has figured out the way.

A thousand years ago, when Xi'an was seven times larger, the two great pagodas and most of the temples were well within the T'ang city wall. Xi'an was the supreme metropolis of the medieval world, unrivaled by Baghdad, surpassing Rome. All the Buddhist temples were allotted their own city block — actually more like a city acre — and Qing Long Si was built on the Xingchang Block in the sixth century. Now it's surrounded by Tian Lumiao Village on a butte at the end of the southern suburbs. There's a fine view of Dayanta to the west and the peaks to the south, slicing China in half. It's a quiet, tranquil site, but there has been plenty of destruction here, too. Everything was rebuilt in 1982.

Qing Long Si is especially important to the Buddhists of Japan. One of their pilgrims, Kobo Daishi, spent the year 805 studying Esoteric Buddhism at the Green Dragon Temple. Four Japanese counties paid for the materials to restore Qing Long Si. The Chinese contributed land and labor. In the main courtyard there's an elaborately carved bei of white marble, a monument to Kobo Daishi.

I find no Buddhist monks in residence or any tourists either. The groundkeeper tells me that the tourists always come on buses; they are always Japanese. To come any other way — by bike or even on foot — is a hard journey, even on a summer day. To reach the temple I must leave the highway, follow a long trail of mud, slick as fish scales, over rolling hills, then walk my bike up the butte.

The Kobo Daishi Thought Hall, the main building which

the keeper unlocks, is more museum than shrine. The walls are filled with paintings and poems depicting Qing Long Si eleven centuries ago. Today it is essentially empty, a collection of fine new buildings and monuments awaiting another group of Buddhist tourists. The spirit of Kobo Daishi has fled forever east; I'm left here.

On my way home the mud between brake pad and tire rim makes stopping impossible. Fortunately, bicycle riders almost never stop in Xi'an. I'm able to ride straight on, eyes down, without injury. Home, I fill a dishpan and go downstairs to uncake the mud, fearful it will otherwise harden into brick overnight, just as the walls and homes of Xi'an have. Dust hardened by water here becomes impervious to water. Only the wind torments it, slow as time; finally even the thickest walls are stung into rubble.

— : : —

The birthplace of Zen, tucked into the present walls of Xi'an, suffered all the ravages of the Cultural Revolution. Now it has barely entered its recovery stage. The founding date of Wo Long Si, the Temple of the Recumbent Dragon, is said to be 520 A.D., no doubt an erroneous citation since it coincides exactly with the appearance of this new school of Buddhism in China.

The Zen temple is a few blocks inside the city wall—by no means easy to find. The entrance is through an unmarked gate and down a long dirt path off Dangting Men Street.

Most of the halls and temples are lost, the frescoes and steles smashed, the legendary library of scrolls unaccounted for, but even in its ruins this is the most active site of

Buddhism I have seen in Xi'an. That is to say two Buddhist monks live here. In addition, some twenty novices from the official Buddhist College in Beijing have been assigned to Wo Long Si. No one has any idea when the new recruits will actually arrive, however, and at present there is no room for them should they accidentally show up. One of the monks ushers us to a sidebuilding which serves as a shrine. There are three cheap plaster Buddhas at its center, their lips red, their eyes white, their faces gold.

Restoration proceeds slowly. The courtyards are a mess. Two of the prayer halls remain standing, but they have been terribly gutted. We don't know how old either is, but neither seems old enough to have housed Wei Guo, the Song dynasty monk who loved to lie down inside. Those passing by dubbed him "the recumbent dragon," a name that's stuck for nine centuries.

Ivan MacLaren points out that the grounds have recently been stripped of heavy industrial equipment. Inside the first prayer hall he can still see massive lathe beds. Beside the second prayer hall is a real antiquity — a stone reflecting pool, an exquisite achievement, with carved figures on its inner rim, all facing upside down to reflect right side up in the blue waters. But the pool is unswept now and drained dark; what is far worse, the carved figures of the pool have been defaced, certainly with a mallet.

In the last building at Wo Long Si, unrestored and unfurnished, two walls missing, we meet a third monk. His name is Lao Lun. He is living under the eaves, having fashioned an outer partition from scraps of wood and twine. Delighted to see us, he insists that we share a cup of hot water. Lao Lun describes himself as a free-lance historical consultant. He wages an independent campaign on myriad fronts: geology, ancient culture, archaeology, literature. "I especially love touring famous places," he declares in textbook English, asking us where we are from and nodding with enthusiasm. "Good to travel," he says, although none of us is traveling at the moment. We've all arrived, in fact, in the exact center of nowhere.

Lao Lun says that during the Cultural Revolution he dug ditches in the mountains south of Xi'an, acting on his own as a protector of religious artifacts. Here, at Wo Long Si, he buried several steles in shallow graves and preserved frescoes by covering them over in mud and straw, building a false wall. Now he lives in a sort of stall, his bedding a straw mat on the floor.

Before we leave, he gives us a stenciled map. It looks like a treasure map, but of what, I can't tell—shrines, statues, steles along a winding road. Lao Lun arranges his inks and with bemused flourishes writes me a poem in the margin. We shake hands and exchange slight bows. We're almost back through the entrance when Sylvia's hand, brushing across a pile of blue roof tiles, dislodges a tin Mao button—dropped, she's sure, by one of the Red Guards and lying in wait for her accidental touch.

— : : —

Sunday we're in search of lamas on the back streets of Xi'an. Little of the modern world's traffic reaches these recesses of the Silk Road, save the occasional jeep or small motorcycle honking its way through the parting seams of a fabric of horse- and human-drawn carts. As each road branches, we keep to the north and west, heading for a corner of the city wall.

We reach a dead end. Straight ahead, there's a factory; on the left, a gate. Sylvia and Ivan ask the children gathered around us where the lama lives. They point at the gate. We wheel our bikes down a narrow passage between brick walls and out into the temple grounds.

The southern half of the courtyard is occupied by a three-story brick building—new apartments. The windows face the Lama Temple squarely, like jury members. The Lama Temple is modest, but graceful; I like its curving lines, its roof cascading over circular red columns, the front partitioned into many doors. Two thin pines flank the main stairway to the temple. The courtyard is paved in stone. Ivan points out the square foundations upon which steles once stood.

The resident lama steps out from a side hall and greets us. He has been practicing Tibetan Buddhism here for fifty years, he says. As a young man he journeyed from Sichuan Province by foot over the Qinling Mountains. There were hundreds of monks in the Xi'an Lamasery in those days; the shrines and prayer halls and living quarters stretched south for blocks. This was the great midway station for pilgrims on the road from Beijing to Lhasa.

The only residents left now are this old monk and one novice. The Red Guards forced the monk to work in the adjoining factory; his young novice is working there still. The old lama is retired. His eyes are glassy with cataracts.

As he speaks, the neighborhood children and a few young

men crowd around, making the monk edgy; nevertheless, he shows us the interior of the temple, unbolting a massive row of doors. The inside is cool and sweet. There are painted statues, shrines with lurid posters, Tibetan deities surrounded by offerings of incense, fruit, and canned peas. Sylvia asks if this is an active shrine; the monk doesn't answer. Only later, when the locals drift away, does he tell us that on new and full moons many still attend services.

It's amazing that the main temple survives whole. Its coffered ceilings, even in the darkness, are a whirl of brightly painted constellations. The lama's quarters, on the other hand, are spartan, to say the least—two hard cots with quilts, one desk, four wooden benches, and in an even smaller room a kitchen with a single-burner coal stove. No New China luxuries: no heat, no running water, no TV, no Sanyo shortwave radio-cassette deck.

The lama has only a single cup; we all share it. The water he serves is boiling hot. He sits on the edge of his cot and answers our questions; first Sylvia translates, then Ivan. He rises once or twice to see who is still watching us from outside. Finally he gets up and shoves the photograph I gave him deep into the desk drawer. It is a snapshot of the Dalai Lama that I slipped into his hand in the temple.

Smiling for the first time, he turns to a framed photograph on the wall, a portrait of the Abbot of the Xi'an Lamasery—the last Abbot, too old to go to the factory, too old to outlive the Cultural Revolution.

When we finish drinking the water, the old lama leads us into the empty courtyard and waits, intent as a deer; then we walk quickly to the first small building behind the temple. He unlocks the door. Inside, there are some scrolls on a table; otherwise, the room is bare. He unlocks a closet door, slides open the back wall—a screen. Behind it are hundreds of bound books heaped high. He hands us volumes at random. They are sutras, some handwritten, others block-printed, each, the lama claims, four hundred years old. I ask if he hid these books here during bad times. No, certain government officials came and moved the entire library to a safe place, Xiaoyanta, the Little Wild Goose Pagoda, many miles to the south, where the sutras could sit out the Cultural Revolution.

We part at the lama's house. He is too tired to walk us to the gate—more worn out than content, more spooked than serene. Piles of books that might never be read again are locked in a windowless room; I think of the lama's sealed eyes. I have no idea what will become of his library. The keeper is old now and poor, too poor to afford so much as a cup of tea for travelers.

— : : —

Xi Wu Tai, the Five Western Terraces, was once a vast collection of Buddhist temples erected on five hills in the heart of Xi'an. Its name is lovely: I dream of pavilions as delicate as any on a T'ang dynasty fan, as phantasmagorical as a Qing landscape; I find myself in streets as ugly as any inside the city walls, not a temple roof in sight.

I am ready to turn back when a young woman offers to guide me to Xi Wu Tai. I follow her into a courtyard, past some houses, and through what appears to be a repair yard for refrigerators. At the end of this alley is a long, broken stairway; at the top, the last surviving pavilion. It is sawed in half, as if by an ocean liner's keel. The southern walls and roof have been hammered down the steep hillside, a heap of beams and broken tiles.

I mount the stairs gingerly and peer into the standing half of this severed shrine, open to the dust and stripped of every last decoration. I can look back down on the blue-gray tiles of a hundred roofs, the halls and pavilions of a vast temple district, now residences and factories, as if Buddhism were abruptly sucked through toothless jaws into a black hole—a crude approximation of the Industrial Revolution.

At the foot of the stairs the woman waits; she guides me back to the courtyard. Someone has removed my bicycle for safekeeping. I'm invited into a two-room home, its floors packed with earth. In the first room is a bed in the corner where an old woman sits up, stares at me, and nods. I drink tea in silence while the woman on the bed studies me.

In the back room I'm shown a small Buddhist shrine. Then I'm led across the courtyard to a much larger shrine. Inside there's a life-size statue of the Buddha and a dozen prayer pillows on the floor. Next door, in a room hardly larger than a closet, I'm invited to stare at a robed woman sitting cross-legged at a high writing desk, chanting sutras from a scroll. She does not once glance up from her recitations. I stare in, embarrassed, and this nun keeps reading aloud in her little room without a window, without a listener; she rocks side to side like an inland sea.

I back away; the door is closed. The old woman on the bed has been helped into the courtyard by her grandchildren; now she leans her weight against a doorjamb and waves to me from the shadow of half a temple, clinging to its littered western terrace like a severed fist.

— : : —

We board the Polish-built bus, which is a half hour late. My students are keyed up for our excursion to Nanwutai. Despite their positions as doctors, none of them has traveled much. Six days a week they are in class; on Sundays, they almost never take it upon themselves to venture off campus.

Now they jockey to sit next to me, as though my very breath bestows fluency in English. Jing Lin-Huang wins out. He tells me what it was like to become a peasant for the first time at the age of sixteen and raise pigs in a village. Stuck in the countryside six years, he was finally chosen to enroll in a biological institute in Wuhan. He studied English on the side there, seven nights a week. His wife and child have stayed behind in Wuhan, of course. Like his classmates, Jing exhibits no curiosity about religion, although it is to a religious site that we are traveling. I tell him the MacLarens, who are sitting up front, and I are trying to become old-fashioned Buddhists, and Jing laughs.

We drive through towns and villages into the wider farmlands south of Xi'an. The bus lurches at each shift, the horn is always pressed. Most of the time we are somewhere in the center of the highway, dodging oncoming traffic, passing the usual bikes and carts, pedestrians and animals. After an hour's hard ride, we reach Taiyigong Village and begin the walk up Nanwutai, a mountain range once terraced by dozens of Buddhist temples.

High humidity makes the trek painful, but the hillsides are green, the air fragrant. After an hour we reach a set of palatial ruins where vendors have spread out their wares under awnings of white sheets. We pause for lunch. Pressed by my students, I sample cold millet soup from a bowl, share their hard-boiled eggs and breads. They buy me a bottle of beer and watch me drink it. They report that the fallen mansion was meant to be the summer home of a local party boss, but that the Red Guards got wind of his hideaway, ransacked it, and drove the old goat through the streets of Xi'an atop a shit wagon. The roofs which clutch these empty interiors seem much older, however, the lines and tiles of a temple.

As we head out for the summit, a peasant in a torn black jacket stops me. He says that he fought the Americans in Korea. Always happy to see foreigners now, he says, though he's obviously seen damn few. All smiles, teeth worn to nubs. His granddaughter, dressed in skirts without a tatter, twirls under a sun umbrella in the ruins.

We arrive on the top of Nanwutai about noon. There's no temple here, just a bare foundation without a name and the scallops of a dirt wall. My students squat on the foundation, stripped to their white undershirts. They remind me of city kids on a school outing in the country. They don't seem to know what to do with themselves. I don't know either.

It is far too hazy to see Xi'an on the northern plain, but on the next peak over I can make out a splendid Buddhist temple. A figure or two moves at its entrance. I've missed out again. The trail that leads to this gutted overlook does not connect to the other southern peaks.

Our bus driver arrives last. He has sprained his ankle quite badly stepping from the bus, but he insisted on walking to the top. His ankle is caved in completely now; he can only hobble a step at a time, and it is clear that he'll not be able to descend unaided. Nevertheless, when some soldiers from the People's Liberation Army arrive to assist, he fights them off. He isn't about to lose face, not this proud idiot, even if we all have to walk back to Xi'an.

The soldiers wrench him a few feet forward; our driver breaks free. Then he stands there, hopelessly immobilized. Every time the soldiers grab him, he screams until they release him. At this rate it will take a week to pull him down the mountain, yet no one is prepared to take responsibility.

Meanwhile, I'm content to consume the whole afternoon descending Nanwutai. The wilderness suggests the North American landscape, which I hadn't thought about until today. I hear our driver bellow in the distance like a moose.

At the foot of Nanwutai the trail flattens. On the other side of a dry creek bed fifty men are quarrying stone. They break off large slabs with axes and chisels and ferry them in tandem to the carvers. They resemble a chain gang; in fact, this could be rehabilitation through hard labor, a common occurrence in this northern province. The quarrymen stop working when they see me. I keep walking. The road is chalked off in sections; small brigades are digging up each plat. Lower down, a team fits paving stones in the trenches. At the bottom are cartloads of crushed stone, icing for the roadbed.

We wait an hour in the village for our recalcitrant driver. My student Jing has located the only phone, a hand-cranked model with a bad connection. My other students are sitting dutifully in the bus, as they sit most of the time in their small rooms. The MacLarens and I decide to tour the village. One never knows what will turn up—a sow coming out the front door of a house; an old peasant woman walking down a back street with a dead dog around her neck.

Then we sit on minuscule benches in the parking lot and purchase clear glasses of tea. The children inspect us. Both Ivan and I have red beards, a pure mark of the Foreign Devil in China. Sylvia has curly locks, almost blonde, nearly as exotic as red. Finally the army arrives with our driver enthroned on a stretcher fashioned from branches and foliage. Still ferocious, he insists on driving. Everyone watches him throw his latest tantrum. He's able to start the engine, but he can't move it a foot. At dusk, a relief driver from the Medical College pulls up in a taxi.

Behind us are the sacred southern terraces, an entire precinct reconverted into what it was before: a land predating Buddhism; a land swallowing up zealots—Mao and monk alike—chewing up the stone of the river, and squeezing out a ribbon of road which disappears beneath its skin like a scar.

— : : —

When I finally return to Wo Long Si one afternoon, hoping to see Lao Lun again, I'm too late. He's disappeared, even his miserable shack behind the meditation hall has been torn down. All that remains is a defaced fresco on a brick wall, plastered with layer upon layer of torn red star posters. The other monks think that Lao Lun might have returned to his old hideout: that is, to Nanwutai. I hope so. It feels better to imagine that he has taken refuge at a monastery, perhaps on that inaccessible terrace I spotted when I was there.

The treasure map he gave me, I see now, is of Nanwutai. It's not the Nanwutai I visited, desolate and in ruins, but Nanwutai in its fullness, Buddhist temples and terraces, monasteries and pagodas, which once commanded the affairs of an Empire, as it still is in the mapmaker's dream.

Tonight, I have a drink with the MacLarens at the Xi'an Hotel. Hanging over the edge of the rooftop bar, I see Xiaoyanta—the Little Wild Goose Pagoda, which I pass by twice a day on my rides into the city. It's another great Buddhist monument from the T'ang, but no worshippers visit it now. It is said that in 1487, an earthquake split Xiaoyanta in half, head to toe, but in 1556, a second jolt zipped it back together. It's a story I'd like to believe, but can't.

This blue-brick pagoda will shrink at dusk and disappear. Then the vast city will wake like a buried self, featureless in the night—streets empty of lights and motors, voice as mute as prayers in a hollow tower. Later, as I walk home, the sweet dust will rise in the darkness from the heated ground, catch in my throat, and render me wordless, too—the way I came in, the way I must go out.

SEEING IN THE DARK

In an afternoon in the dead-center of summer the train drops from the Qinling Mountain Range and returns on time to Xi'an, where one of the most beautiful train stations in China has just been torn down. There is always something being torn down and something else being put up everywhere, everywhere. At the station the next round of passengers, mostly peasants who have sold their wares in the city, collect under a temporary shelter.

The person I was to meet is not on the train. I wait until the platform is empty. When I struggle back onto a #5 Bus, mumble my destination, and pay the ticket-taker two mao, it is dark. We chug along the boulevards, overtaking families on foot, on bikes, on a few rattling rototillers hitched to wagons.

It has long been believed in China that headlights blind oncoming traffic. In practice, this belief creates possibilities for mayhem undreamt of anywhere else in the paved world. At major intersections the #5 bus headlights snap on once or twice, then off. Completely off. We are all traveling in the dark. We travel in the dark constantly.

I am thinking of the time when Fred and I left the Shaanxi opera early. It was dusk as we unlocked our bikes, freeing the wooden tickets and handing them to the parking lot attendant on our way out. It was warm, too. It was, in fact, the heart of the Xi'an summer, one of those blessed days when hard rain had not turned the silty margins to soup. We pedaled side by side down Dong Dajie, circled the silent Bell Tower, and headed south. Bicycles crisscrossed the intersections at random, bells cackling like wild geese in a mist. Outside the seven-mile city wall, we crossed a moat into the unlit suburbs, overtaking pedestrians in white shirttails and then a donkey cart, its drum full of night soil scooped by hand from the city latrines. The last wide boulevard leading to the Medical College was deserted and darker still.

We stopped speaking and strained to see ahead impossible without street lights. An old woman was walking on the wrong side of the road. She was pushing a cabbage cart straight at us. We could not see her. We could not see her coming at us on the wrong side of the road and yet, at the last moment, we swerved — we swerved together for reasons we will never discover — and we missed her by inches. We listened as her cart wheels plod into the distance behind us; we coasted for a moment, taking a long breath; and we didn't speak.

There was nothing to say then. Perhaps we thought: only someone severely deranged would dare drive on these streets after dark—as we often did—where pedestrians and beasts of burden wandered aimlessly and even machinery refused to use its headlights.

It never made sense, that willful lack of light. The sheer bulk of time in isolation has made China a world unto itself—a world forever in the dark, forever tearing itself to pieces, which is also the secret of its continuity. It's a continuity punctuated with violence, always subject to a sudden shift to the opposite extreme.

THE TAO
AVERAGES

When the Chinese Cultural Revolution began in 1966, half the structures at Ba Xian An, the Temple of the Eight Immortals, were hammered back into the earth by the Red Guards. For a thousand years, this had been the largest Taoist monastery in Xi'an. Today even those few remaining buildings are gutted and closed, the courtyard of Ba Xian An bisected by new apartments and a machine factory.

Ba Xian An is a mile east of the Xi'an city wall, and its only entrance is a small gate on a side street. Tonight is a new moon, and I am surprised to find Taoist services in full swing. Within the cramped courtyard I count twenty dark-robed monks, their heads shaven. Three are said to be young novices. Although the monks assure me that there are no women in their ranks, I notice two Taoist nuns emerging briefly from a back building.

The worshippers, mostly elderly, kneel down to burn likenesses of paper money, perhaps Bank of Hell notes which, once rendered into smoke, waft into the land of the dead where relatives and ancestors are ever in need of cash. One majestic monk stands at the top of the temple stairs and casts firecrackers into the crowd. There is no discernible order in the service. Singing, clanging of wooden sticks, shouting of prayers and chants echo the din of holy chaos, Taoism as it has been for centuries.

Still, the grounds of Ba Xian An are those of a factory — not of a temple — paved, walled, and pinched into an obscure corner of these faceless suburbs, and it is difficult to imagine what was once here: the spacious monastery and nunnery, the halls and shrines and temples. At the turn of the century, Ba Xian An was much favored by the rulers of China. When the Imperial Court at Beijing was driven into exile and retreated to the ancient capital, Cixi, the last Empress of China, often visited Ba Xian An with her sketchbook to paint its famous peonies.

There is not a single peony left now, and few gardens in the whole of outer Xi'an. The Temple of the Eight Immortals, severed from nature and its past, has been absorbed by the industries of a new China.

— : : —

Taoism originated in China, perhaps as early as 770 B.C., centuries before Buddhists and Christians and Moslems were entrenched, centuries before the oldest empire on earth got its official start in the Wei Valley. From the first, the Taoists sought harmony not with society, the state, or the gods, but with nature. They rejected discipline and obedience, accepting only Tao, the Way, the pure flow of existence itself.

This cultivation of natural forces, with its allegiance to personal visions, meant that early Taoism had no formal organizations, elaborate rituals, or pantheon of deities, but its esoteric elements soon lent themselves to the formulation of complex and fantastic rites—eventually to the establishment of shrines and temples, the writing of texts, and the building of monasteries.

It's their ruins that remain here, ironically because the central goal of the Taoists was the attainment of endless physical life—a real immortality. Because the body was of nature and nature did not cease, Taoists reasoned that men and women need not cease either, provided they remained in natural harmony. That was the stickler. To come into natural harmony, we require an elixir from nature.

The early Taoists scoured the countryside for these precious substances. Emperor Qin was said to have sampled all the elixirs of Xi'an, and for good reason: he feared death by invasion or revolution the moment he took the throne. Many of his measures were defensive, from finishing the Great Wall to fortifying the roads to his 270 palaces (each an exact copy of those he had razed in the course of unifying China), but once secure from mortal enemies, he took on mortality itself. The Taoists insisted that the only genuine elixir of life was an herb grown in the midst of the Eastern Sea, on Mount P'eng-lai—most likely this was Japan, since the magical isle was said to recede in ocean swells as one approached it. The emperor sent an expedition of youths, male and female, to the east, but they never returned. Finally he set out himself in a long caravan to the east and died en route, of natural causes as it were, 1650 li (530 miles) from Xi'an. His attendants drew the curtains over his caravan to conceal his demise, and to forestall chaos until he could reach his great mausoleum; but all along the road they smelled him coming.

Qin's eventual successors, the rulers of the Han dynasty, kept their capital at Xi'an. Claiming to possess Spirit Fungus, that elusive elixir of life, Taoist sorcerers and alchemists secured prominent political positions. Some remained hermits, but Taoism was becoming an institution, as every movement in China must to survive. It was declared the official religion of the empire in 444 A.D. From that period on, Taoist priests presided over autonomous districts, and a formal monastic life began. Under the first T'ang emperor (who fancied himself a direct descendant of Taoism's founder), monasteries and convents routinely ordained and certified members, who were exempt from taxation and military conscription.

Although the most powerful mystical force in state affairs for centuries, Taoism has left few traces in its capital, but Sylvia and Ivan MacLaren have dug up a few obscure references, as usual, including a temple said to be where Taoism was born. The problem is how to get there.

— : : —

Lou Guan Tai, meaning High View Terrace, forty-seven miles southwest of Xi'an, is honored throughout China as the "original place" of Taoism. The Red Guards spent considerable resources to storm this citadel in the Qinling Mountains. They razed buildings and removed a statue of Lao Zi, the founder of Taoism. But even then the monks refused to leave Lou Guan Tai, where their ancestors had worshipped for two thousand years, where we found them worshipping today.

My students have arranged another excursion by bus, south again, this time to the foothills of Lou Guan Tai. By chance, it is precisely where the MacLarens and I want to go as we retrace the Way. For my students, however, nature seems to be the attraction. The southern hills are forested in ancient bamboo terraces, fracturing light into a labyrinth of color.

From the bamboo shafts and foliage, Yin Xi (also know as Zhou Da Fu) built a celestial observatory here during the Zhou dynasty. His pavilion was called the Observation Tower of Grass. Yin Xi tended it in seclusion until one day he met Lao Zi at the base of this peak; afterwards, he erected a scripture-teaching platform from which he began the transmission of Tao to the Chinese. This is the story. In fact, no one even knows whether Lao Zi is real or imagined. Still, the writings ascribed to him constitute one of the great sacred texts of the world, and Lou Guan Tai has become the formal starting point of the Way.

At the summit of Lou Guan Tai, we find no tower of grass, no sacred pulpit, but neither do we find the ruins we expected. Instead, Lou Guan Tai is restored. It's the first complete Taoist complex we've come across at Xi'an.

The temple grounds overlook a deep valley in the midst of an unpopulated range of green mountains. Some thirty monks—twenty elders and ten novices—are now in residence. We are guided into the main temple by a loquacious seventy-year-old monk who came to Lou Guan Tai from Tai Bai Shan twenty-five years ago. Standing before an altar in the main temple, between statues of Yin Xi and Lao Zi, he tells his version of Taoism's birth.

One day, he says, Yin Xi sighted a red cloud in the east. He knew it heralded the arrival of an important man, for the cloud was in the shape of a dragon and also of a serpent. Yin Xi walked to the base of the mountain; there he met a traveler, a man mounted backwards on a cow—it was Lao Zi. Lao Zi was heading westward in search of firewood. (Great men, the monk tells my students, always travel east to west.) Desiring to talk at length with Lao Zi, Yin Xi tried to stop him by grabbing the tail of his cow. He was dragged fifty-three steps on his knees until Lao Zi, admiring his pluck, agreed to talk. They went to the summit together. There Lao Zi initiated Yin Xi into the rites of Taoism. He revealed the Nine Hundred Principles of the Way, presented Yin Xi with the sacred text, Tao De Jing ("The Way and Its Power"), from which Yin could instruct others, and fashioned a grinding stone for the preparation of the elixir of life. Then Lao Zi descended Lou Guan Tai, remounted his cow, and rode into the sunset.

The old monk adds that Lao Zi emerged from his mother's womb with a full head of white hair and spoke in complete sentences from the hour of his birth. My students make great sport of these stories—prodding the monk, laughing out loud. Although several of them have lived in the countryside during the Cultural Revolution, they hold rural people in great disdain, perhaps even in terror.

In the rear courtyard we are shown a grinding stone in an

iron cage, the one Lao Zi used. Xian dan, the elixir of life, is still prepared there. Some of the monks at Lou Guan Tai continue other old practices, too: those of the hygiene school. According to its tenets, the physical form of life endures indefinitely so long as the inner and outer harmonies are maintained. To avoid contamination of the inner world of the body, however, adherents have to develop extreme programs of dieting, fasting, and breathing. The goal is to seal off the body completely, to live on one's own breath and saliva.

Of course, as even the most accomplished Taoist monks eventually die off, some alterations in the original hygiene movement have been inevitable. The concept of an immortal embryo, born in the human body, eventually gained acceptance. This deeper self, still a physical entity, can be nourished by the proper regimen. Then, when the outer body dies, the inner body emerges to wander the universe in perfect freedom. Hence, the continuing appearance of the Immortals in Taoist tradition.

The most famous of the Han dynasty rulers, Wu Ti (140–87 B.C.), is said to have believed in this deeper body. He assisted in the Taoist experiments of his time—the most common, an attempt to transform cinnabar into gold. The emperor's mentor was the monk Li Shao-chin. When Li died, a fellow monk wrote that this master had avoided eating cereals and therefore escaped old age; even at his death, he was transformed. When his tomb was opened several years later, followers found only an empty cap and robe.

The Taoists have formulated a cosmology as elaborate as that of the Buddhists. The human body is a universe in miniature. Its three centers are the head, the chest, and the stomach, and within each center are fields of cinnabar where 36,000 gods preside. The same 36,000 gods also rule the outside world. Each center of the body is subdivided into compartments. The supreme god lives in the ninth compartment of the head; adjacent is a kind of bookkeeper who registers a person as mortal or immortal. To have one's name inscribed in the register of the Immortals, however, one has to keep all 36,000 gods happy, no easy task because they are known to despise the odor of meat and the aroma of wine. Cereal grains are an anathema, too, since the death-dealing worms in the cinnabar feed on grains. Masters of inner hygiene are required to achieve a complete fast. In the most esoteric version of this fast, followers join their breath with their semen to produce and nurture the growth of a pure embryonic body.

The monks at Lou Guan Tai, to whatever extent they pursue these esoteric avenues, are yet of this world. Precisely at noon they descend the fifty-three steps to their dining hall. Time for lunch and nap. Like workers all over China, the monks at Lou Guan Tai have made the long midday break part of their religion. My students, amused by this exodus, dub them the monks who punch the clock.

— : : —

On our way down Lou Guan Tai we Westerners insist on turning off the main trail to inspect a pagoda we spotted on the way up. Only one of my students, Jing, decides to accompany us. The rest go dutifully back to the bus. The path to the pagoda runs through the heart of several earthen villages where piglets are parked by the front doors like family dogs. The pagoda proves to be a large octagon in the T'ang dynasty style. Its most curious aspect is the way it leans north toward Xi'an at an angle as severe as that of the Tower of Pisa.

On each eave the grasses have taken root; the peak of the pagoda is a thick thatch of weeds and straw. A peasant living nearby can tell us nothing about its history, not even its name, but he is willing to take us to the top for a fee. The inner stairs appear unsafe, however, so after a look into the dark interior, we turn back, strolling the margin between the bamboo uplands and lowlands of wheat.

At the main road we meet a peasant woman walking a small rabbit. She has tied a leash of twine to its back foot. She is selling stuffed animals decorated with pieces of discarded foil. Although her wares are not exquisite by folk standards, their price is a pittance, and I don't haggle as I usually do in the streets of Xi'an. She leaves with my money, singing, her rabbit in tow.

Our way home is slowed by sheaves of wheat which the peasants have heaped high on the road in hopes that the passing trucks and buses will do the threshing.

— : : —

Just inside the eastern gates of Xi'an is a Taoist temple dedicated to the cult of Tai Shan. Animal sacrifices were made here to the Immortals residing on Mount Tai. Only two buildings survived the plunderings of the Red Guards. Both are shackled with heavy chains and padlocks.

The temple's name is Dong Yue Miao, the Eastern Peak Temple. It was founded late, in 1116 A.D., and served its followers for a mere nine centuries. When the Red Guards tore open the doors to the east wing, they found a great treasure in the Palace of Three Religions (San Jiao Gong): the statues of Lao Zi, Buddha, and Confucius, which the Ming rulers erected here as if to unite these three ancient rivals. This triumvirate was swiftly ground into dust.

Absolutely nothing has been restored since. Dong Yue Miao is like a monument to the Cultural Revolution. The one temple and the one pavilion which remain are surrounded by the classrooms of a primary school. I cannot persuade the officials to unlock the doors. They tell me that they do not have the authority. The children follow me back and forth between the buildings.

Dong Yue Miao was celebrated for the frescoes on its inner walls. I peer into the darkness, pressing against the unhinged and battered doors, and after several minutes I make out the contours of a landscape and human figures. The frescoes have been horribly defaced; a storm of hammers and chisels is imprinted on the wall.

Disappointed, I push my bicycle out of the school yard and stop under the eastern arch of the Ming city wall. Brigades of corvée laborers are layered across the banks below the wall, digging out the old city moat by hand. Their shovels form a relay up the banks. No machinery in this hole. As many as thirty thousand men and women surround the city on their single day of rest. In ten years, the project will be done, the moat excavated and restored to its original depth, the banks bricked to match the walls, and water will once again ring this city, its four cardinal gates and its archers' towers.

In the digging of that great ditch, in the lines of curious schoolchildren who examine me as I scrutinize the ruined interiors of a shrine through long cracks in broken doors, I first feel that the true body of China has escaped the prison of its ruins; that the very ruins are themselves the lost Way.

THE
RUBBING
MASTER

The Provincial Museum is housed in the old Temple of Confucius, which dates from 1374 A.D. It contains the great treasures of Old China from the late and early dynasties all the way back to the Stone Age. Dusty, ill-lit, poorly organized, it is my favorite museum on earth.

At its heart is Bei Lin—the Forest of Steles—the premier collection of engraved stone tablets in China. The largest single grove consists of the Confucian Classics, and occupies its own gallery: 114 double-sided stone blocks. Most of what has survived the successive incarnations of Xi'an had to be buried in the earth or cast into stone: the terra-cotta warriors and royal tumuli; the pagodas and temple steles of the Han and T'ang; the pottery, the broken tiles, the bone.

This is the running text of those ruins; the Confucians deserve credit that it survives at all. They were the preservers, the collectors. From feudalism to socialism, China has remained a Confucian empire. Peasants may have prayed to ancestors and spirits far longer and in greater numbers, workers may have revered the patron and city gods with more zeal, but the scholars and bureaucrats have shaped China from the top. If Taoism or Buddhism or Christianity were necessary to address the wild and esoteric longings of the secret heart and mind, Confucianism took care of the rest, of what counted—the practical, the ethical, the material, the humdrum harmonies of family and society, the whole enmeshed hierarchy.

Confucius was a fifth century B.C. reactionary; he derived his wisdom from much older models. His teachings were concentrated on individual conduct and mass synchronization—the two are inseparable. His approach led to the elaboration of a ponderous state bureaucracy perpetuated by a rigorous system of examinations. The individual's every outward act was always under the microscope, a maze of lenses increasingly powerful and distant. By the time of his death in 479 B.C., Confucius had already been honored with the first temple built in his name. Two centuries later, his followers were numerous enough to feel the full wrath of Emperor Qin; their schools were closed, their books burned, their Sage denounced. A thousand temples to Confucius were to flourish after the first emperor died. The Imperial Examinations lasted well into the twentieth century; Confucian education and bureaucracy are still with us now.

The Temple of Confucius at Xi'an survived, however, only because its conversion to a museum came soon after the revolution, in 1952. Within its halls are bronzes and jades from the Zhou dynasty; plumbing pipes, a south-pointing chariot, and the world's first seismograph from the immediate successors of Emperor Qin; tricolored horses and scraps of silk from the days of the T'ang; and more than a thousand steles from every period, first gathered together in Xi'an in 1090 A.D.

The center of this stone library has always been the Confucian Classics, carved at Xi'an in 837 A.D.; like a bureaucracy of magical winches and cleats, it has anchored China to the center of its own world for centuries, and does so still.

— : : —

To foreigners, however, the heart of the Forest of Steles is not the Confucian Classics, that petrified Encyclopedia Sinica, but a single tablet, the Nestorian Stele, which records the arrival of Christianity in China in 635 A.D. and its progress in the capital during the seventh and eighth centuries.

The Nestorian tablet is nine feet tall, a yard wide, a foot thick, and weighs two tons. It is composed of limestone as black as a cast-iron lamppost and rests on a tortoise-shaped base. The rounded peak is finely carved: a cross floats in a lotus cloud with two flowering shrubs. Atop the cross is a massive pearl, held by a phantasmagorical figure described variously as a fish monster or crocodile. The cross has been set within a triangle. Immediately beneath is a matrix of nine characters, an inscription reading "The Monument Commemorating the Propagation of the Luminous Religion (Da Qin) in the Middle Kingdom."

The polyglot text is inscribed in long columns: 1900 characters in Chinese, 50 words in Syriac, 72 names of Christian priests and functionaries in the old Estrangela script. The

history it relates was composed in 781 A.D. by a local priest
of the Da Qin monastery. His Chinese name is Ching-Ching;
in Syrian, he is called Adam, pope of Zhinastan.

The story begins with an evocation of the Christian God,
the "One who is true and firm, who, being Uncreated, is the
Origin of Origins, who is ever Incomprehensible and Invisible, yet everywhere mysteriously existing to the Last of
Lasts." The explication of doctrine on the Nestorian Stele
employs phrases and concepts from a wide range of Chinese
sources — Taoism, Buddhism, and the Confucian Classics —
but the main thrust is clearly Christian.

The creation of the world recounted there recalls the ac-
count in *Genesis;* man is a fallen giant who in yielding to
Satanic temptations suffers confusion and darkness; the
Messiah who came to earth "took an oar in the Vessel of
Mercy and ascended to the Palace of Light, whereby all
rational beings were conveyed across the Gulf."

The priests and ministers of this Luminous Religion in China
kept no slaves, accumulated no wealth, fasted frequently, worshipped seven times a day, and made a bloodless sacrifice once
a week. They were bearded and bald. The first Nestorian mis-
sionary to reach the gates of the capital was Alopen. He was
met by Duke Fang. The sutras he carried were translated, and
the T'ang Emperor T'ai-Tsung studied the new faith in his
"Forbidden Apartments." Convinced of its "correctness," the
emperor issued an imperial decree. As copied out on the
Nestorian Stele, it is a model of Chinese tolerance:

The Way had not, at all times and in all places, the
selfsame name; the Sage had not, at all times and in all

places, the selfsame human body. Heaven caused a suitable religion to be instituted for every region and clime so that each one of the races of mankind might be saved. Bishop Alopen of the Kingdom of Da Qin [Christendom], bringing with him the sutras and images, has come from afar and presented them to our Capital. Having carefully examined the scope of his teaching, we find it to be mysteriously spiritual and of silent operation. Having observed its principal and most essential points, we reached the conclusion that they cover all that is most important in life. Their language is free from perplexing expressions; their principles are so simple that they remain as the fish would remain even after the net were forgotten. This teaching is helpful to all creatures and beneficial to all men. So let it have free course throughout the Empire.

A Da Qin monastery was immediately built in the I-ning Ward of Xi'an; twenty-one priests were ordained there, and a portrait of the patron Emperor of Christianity in China was painted on its walls.

— : : —

Succeeding emperors of the T'ang generally tolerated the Nestorians. Christian monasteries were built in every prefecture and province of the Middle Kingdom. With the ascension of the infamous Empress Wu, however, the Taoists were able to strike down their foreign rivals. For a generation, the altars of the Nestorian churches lay smashed. Not until 744 A.D., when a missionary named Chi-Ho reached Xi'an and converted the new emperor to the Nestorian Way, were the monasteries rebuilt. Then worshippers flocked to their Luminous Shrines which received royal tributes as great as "the highest peaks of the highest mountains in the south." They wore the shining feathers of the kingfisher and no longer looked or felt themselves foreign, but after a century in China, no one is left who is not very Chinese. Even the Jews who came here were absorbed utterly.

Royal favor rained upon the Christians for generations, and they gave their allegiance to the emperor. "The whole Universe receives life and light because of him," the Stele proclaims. And so the Nestorians settled themselves quietly and contentedly and firmly into the Chinese nation, worshipping at Xi'an for some 219 years until a single imperial edict, issued by Emperor Wu-Tsung in 845 A.D., abruptly ended the progress of Christianity in China.

It is the reverse of the edict which welcomed the first Nestorians at the western gate two centuries earlier, and could have been penned by Chairman Mao:

Wasting human labor (in building shrines); plundering the people's purse (to buy temple decorations); ignoring Imperial contributions (and decrees); neglecting both husband and wife (by requiring strange vigils)—no teaching is more pernicious. . . . How dare the insignificant Teaching of Western Lands compete with ours? Once established, these strange customs have been allowed to prevail far and wide, in a degenerate age, but now the people are soaked to the bone and the national spirit is unconsciously spoiled.

The masses were asked to help dispense justice: "We have finally decided to put an end to such conspicuous evils. Do ye, Our subjects, at home and abroad, obey and conform to Our sincere will. If ye send in a Memorial suggesting how to exterminate these evils which have beset Us for many Dynasties, We shall do all We can to carry out the plan."

The plan of the people was simple — rehabilitation through labor: "As to those monks and nuns who teach the religions of foreign countries, we command that they return to secular life and cease to confuse our national customs and manners."

Eliminating all sources of spiritual pollution, China once again drew into itself: "More than a hundred thousand idle, lazy people and busybodies have been driven off, and numberless beautifully decorated useless temples have been completely swept away. Hereafter, purity of life shall rule Our people. . . ."

The persecutions of 845 were extreme and thorough, a model of xenophobic action. By the end of the ninth century, it was said that only one Christian remained in China; the Nestorian Stele disappeared from the face of the earth.

— : : —

Eight centuries after the Great Persecutions, in about the year 1625, the Nestorian Stele was unearthed outside the city walls of Xi'an.

This discovery coincided with the reappearance of Christian missionaries in China. A few of them, primarily Jesuits, traveled through Xi'an during this period and saw the Nestorian Stele for themselves. The tablet was in superb condition, which suggests it had been buried since the end of the T'ang dynasty, like thousands of holy relics, for protection, then completely forgotten — as forgotten as the Christians of China.

The first rubbing of the Nestorian inscription was sent to Dr. Leon Li, a Chinese Christian living in Hangzhou; the first translation, into Latin, quickly followed. Meanwhile, the Stele was moved closer to Xi'an — to a Buddhist temple a mile outside the western gate. The Moslems razed this temple during the Islamic Revolt of 1862, but they did not touch the Nestorian Stele.

In the fall of 1907, workmen undertook to move it inside the city for the first time; the reason was the arrival of an art collector from the West. Rumor says he offered 3000 taels for the stele and that he intended to ship it to the British Museum, where it would be placed beside the Rosetta Stone. The Governor of Shaanxi Province intervened; he ordered the stone to be hauled to the Temple of Confucius for safekeeping. A tortoise foundation was carved for it in the Forest of Steloo. On October 2, 1907, the Nestorian Stele reached its present location.

The would-be purchaser of 1907 was actually a Dr. Frits Holm from Denmark. When he could not procure the original stele, he ordered a full-scale replica to be cut from limestone in Xi'an. Once cut, it had to be transported overland 350 miles in a special cart to what was then the nearest railway station, Cheng-chou. Red tape kept even the Nestorian Stele's replica in China for another year. On February 28, 1908, it was shipped from Shanghai and on June 16, it was deposited in the Metropolitan Museum of Art in New York City "as a loan." According to Dr. Holm, the replica was an exquisite work in its own right, perhaps one of the last great steles crafted in China.

The Stele stands as much for the disappearance as for the arrival of Christianity in China. Francis Nichols, who saw the Nestorian monument in 1902, a few years before it was carried into the city proper, made the key observation in *Through Hidden Shensi* (New York: Scribner's and Sons, 1905): "Like every other foreign-born influence that has been left to itself to battle with the traditional conservatism of Shensi, the Christianity of the eighth century was simply dissolved in its environment as easily as the waters of a spring might lose themselves in the sands of the desert."

And within a few years, Nichols himself dissolved into the deserts of China, dying of pneumonia in southern Tibet eighteen months after he "left New York with the plan of penetrating Tibet to Lhasa, then still the mysterious and unvisited city." Nichols came within a hundred miles of Lhasa. He was my age exactly, thirty-six, when he died, and he found China pitiless.

— : : —

I've been giving the Nestorian Stele plenty of thought this week, rifling through old books. Rick Wacker's given me another translation of the Nestorian Stele. Fred has an odd-ball study he picked up in Japan. Nobody really cares what I discover, of course. They're just humoring me. Dr. Fu thinks I'm crazy. I've become a mole. Maybe that's what China means to make of me in the end.

Last night I reached some conclusions.

"Early in the year 1625," writes A.C. Moule, in *Christians*

in China Before the Year 1550 (New York: Macmillan,
1930), "perhaps about the beginning of March, trenches
were being dug for the foundations of some building near the
district town of Chou-chih, thirty or forty miles to the west
of the city of Hsi-an, when the workmen came upon a great
slab of stone buried seven feet beneath the surface of the
ground." It was the Nestorian Stele. According to the Chinese version, they were not digging a foundation but a grave
that day. The governor's favorite child, a devout Buddhist,
was about to be buried, and the child's spirit was believed to
have guided the gravediggers to the holy monument.

Exactly where the Nestorian Stele was buried or where it
stood in the eighth and ninth centuries, no one can say; but it
was not within the walls of Xi'an. P.Y. Saeki, a Japanese
scholar, has made the most detailed inquiry. He argues in
The Nestorian Documents and Relics in China (Tokyo:
Maruzen, 1951) that the Stele first stood and was subse-
quently hidden in the ground southwest of Xi'an at Lou
Guan Tai—specifically, on a middle slope in a place called
Wu-chun, where in 756 A.D. the T'ang Emperor Su-tsung
built a Nestorian monastery.

I don't doubt that Lou Guan Tai, by tradition the birthplace of Taoism in China, was also the location of a
Nestorian monastery and, ultimately, the original site of the
buried Stele. *The Topographical Book of Chou-chih,* written
in 1563, certainly confirms the existence of a Nestorian
monastery "in the middle of the hillside which forms a table-
land of the Tower Valley." Moreover, in the same place there
also stood a pagoda, "an eight-cornered one, seventy or
eighty-feet-high, originally built by the imperial orders of

Emperor T'ai-tsung," who welcomed the first Christian mis-sionary to China. This is the leaning pagoda that I saw myself when I visited Lou Guan Tai. It predates the Nestorian Stele, to which it is intimately linked, by a full century.

In 1933, four Chinese scholars spent a night in the Taoist Temple at Lou Guan Tai. From there, according to Saeki they happened to see below them "a Tower rising high into the sky at the foot of the hill." In the morning, they went down to it. A villager told them that the ruins around this pagoda had an old name — Da Qin Si. It was the Nestorian monastery — a temple complex of the Luminous Faith of Rome.

Not much was left, even in 1933; but an iron bell cast in 1444, which once hung from the western eaves of the monas-tery, contained an inscription confirming that the temple was built by order of the T'ang Emperor. The scholars also found a stone tablet describing a Throne of Buddha; in the eigh-teenth century, they point out, this monastery served as a Buddhist temple. In fact, the complex survived as long as it did only by undergoing various incarnations, serving as the vessel of successive religions after the Nestorians disap-peared, until there were no religions left. In this way, the pagoda might be said to represent the progress of all religions in China.

The chief remains of what was perhaps the first Christian monastery in China is the leaning pagoda at Lou Guan Tai. This is the only structure left. The scholars who visited there in 1933 were struck by its resemblance to the Great Wild Goose Pagoda in Xi'an. Farmers in the region believed that the Da Qin Pagoda was built of stone left over from the building of that most famous of all T'ang dynasty towers.

Those scholars were also able to climb to the top despite the poor condition of the tower's interior. On the second story and the third, they saw clay images of Kuan-Yin, the Goddess of Mercy, in a style dating from the T'ang or Sung dynasty. On the seventh story, they made rubbings of the characters carved over the archways on the south and the west. These were later found to be Tibetan writings, including a six-character Lamaist charm.

All the faiths that once resided at Xi'an are entangled in the history of the Nestorian Stele, first erected in the shadow of this ruined tower of the T'ang; buried there in 845 A.D. when the Christians were expelled from their monasteries; forgotten after a few generations; rediscovered by the sheerest accident, in 1625, in the same way that, by happenstance, the First Emperor's treasures were returned to the surface in our time. What more do these loesslands conceal? Plenty, no doubt. Every block of this desolate plain is monumental.

A further odd note:

On September 21, 1911, the Honorable Mrs. Gordon of Ireland, caused a second replica of the Nestorian Stele to be placed upon the summit of Mt. Koya in Japan. It was on Mt. Koya that Kobo Daishi (Kang Hai), the pilgrim who came to Xi'an in 804, founded the monastery of Kongo-buji upon his return to Japan in 816—and also where he preached the tenets of a new sect of Buddhism, Shingonbu. This became the largest Buddhist sect in Japan. The peak still attracts thousands of Japanese pilgrims each year. This is also the location of the Okuno-in Cemetery, where the dead by the thousands, emperors included, are buried in expectation of the coming of Miroku, a Buddhist Messiah. Within this messianic Buddhist cemetery—with its varied Xi'an connections—stands the reproduced Nestorian Stele, like a fetish.

There is only this to add:

A certain pictorial stele at Xi'an is engraved with the journey of Emperor Hung Wu, founder of the Ming dynasty, up the holy peak of Hua Shan. Francis Nichols described this stele in these words:

> The picture of the sacred mountain, as it was indelibly stamped on Hung Wu's memory, was carved on a stone tablet in the yard of the temple at the base of the mountain. The white dotted line is the winding, difficult trail up the mountain-side. The figure of a man in the various stages of the ascent is Hung Wu in the garb of an ordinary pilgrim. The white spots represent the course of the rabbit which was the Emperor's guide in his dream-pilgrimage.

It hasn't escaped my attention—holed up as I am in this vault with nothing but memory and cement—that it was on the slopes of Lou Guan Ti, returning from the Da Qin pagoda, that I chanced upon an old woman leading a rabbit by a string. No doubt it was the emperor's rabbit, sent for me or at the very least, an odd coincidence of displacement which, in the pagan mind, connects mountain to mountain, stone to stone, making the ruins of these various religions one.

— : : —

On my final visit to the Temple of Confucius and its Forest of Steles, I enter at the south gate, a passage once reserved for the emperor and the number one scholar of the realm. I observe a rubbing master at work on a series of stone tablets.

The rubbing master is transcribing the stone carvings to inked paper. Tamping with his wooden mallet until the tracing sheet is firmly mounted, stripping off the scroll, then wrapping up his tools with great care, he proceeds from commission to commission. I merely follow. The tablets are jet black with rubbing ink, their indented texts worn and defaced from centuries of copy. The process has not changed in a thousand years, but demand has fallen off. The mallets are often silent; most of the rubbings these days are made in downtown Xi'an, a block north of the Friendship Store, in a factory where metal forms of the original steles are used to make impressions.

I move in tandem with the rubbing master. Twice a year, on the fall and spring equinoxes, the Confucian gentlemen of old Xi'an would slaughter a cow and sprinkle its hot blood on the altar that once stood at the entrance to these grounds. A decade ago, their descendants passed by here in dunce caps, eyes cast to the ground—Professor Zhong among them, perhaps. Those fallen scholars might have had in mind their Sage's dictum—to remain true to oneself in the era of a bad Prince—but there's a point at which even a sage can't go on.

The rubbing master stops at the stele of Da Ma, the Buddhist pilgrim to China. His hair in ringlets, his earlobes weighted down with circular baubles, Da Ma contemplates a bowl of incense in the shape of a cup of saki; instead of wearing his halo, he sits upon it. Some say Da Ma introduced

Buddhism to Japan; others say his likeness is actually that of a Chinese Jew; a Jesuit missionary insists that Da Ma is St. Thomas the Apostle in disguise. But all these identifications are pure piss-water. Good God, no apostle ever stood on this piece of the earth, I'm sure of it.

Quite sure: Xi'an is too weighed down, too full of misery, to ever be a source of happiness. There's nothing on either side of the great screen now. Even on the other side there's only a blank stone without a single line of calligraphy on its face.

I hear the mallet in another room, pounding shoulder-high on a black plate.

CHINESE TV

Strolling the campus tonight, I skirt a dozen families standing in a grassless courtyard transfixed by a TV screen mounted on a pedestal. They are watching cartoons, everything from "The Pigsy Eats Melons" to "Ding Dong Fights the Monkey King"—ghost images of our beloved "Kukla, Fran, and Ollie" driven through the center of the earth.

It's as if four decades of television start over again here—and I am pushed back to the fifties before Uncle Miltie, before Lucy, before Ozzie and Harriet and David and Ricky. Even in China, TV is the world. I have my own 25″ Telefunken color console parked in the living room; Professor Zhong has his, too, a tiny, browbeaten black-and-white TV from Poland.

Everytime I turn on my set it's like waking up at the dawn of the Television Age on another planet, quite possibly in another galaxy. With a choice of two, sometimes three government networks, I can switch from a bombastic travelogue ("Across Our Motherland") to a regional opera ("Forced to Go to the Exam"), from popular science ("Uses of Potatoes") to home economics ("Prevention of Moth Damage to Woolen Clothing"). This week I've watched "Cafe Karnak" from Egypt; last night I fell asleep in my own overstuffed chair in the midst of a Romanian masterpiece, "Cyanide and Raindrops." My favorite series, of course, is a kung fu epic imported from Hong Kong in which the hero, Huo Yuanjia, eventually loses to the evildoers of Tianjin during the Opium Wars. I have seen enough episodes to memorize the theme, "The Great Wall Never Falls," which I whistle as I ride through the streets. It never fails to shake up those I overtake, when they realize that the whistler is a foreign devil.

The 7:00 P.M. newscast has taught me how to count in Chinese; the weather forecast at the end is a roll call of clearly enunciated temperatures for the major cities of China — it's my litany.

The opening news shot, I've noticed, is nearly always of the interior of the Great Hall of the People — who's come today to pay tribute? The communist regime holds court nightly — a stripped-down version of the old T'ang dynasty. I've memorized every antimacassar on every overstuffed chair in the room. The two delegations of the day are seated in a single fan-shaped line, Chinese on one side, foreigners on the other, their two leaders meeting at the centerpoint, cuspidors at their feet like obedient palace dogs.

This is the news I've come to love, even if I understand nothing. Factory workers and pig farmers are national news, while the world outside is dim and fragmented: clips of a riot in London, a bombing in Beirut, a subway massacre in New York City. I have a diminishing notion of what is happening beyond these borders. I'd rather see a cabbage farmer in Harbin any day or a washing machine factory foreman in Guangzhou than another mass murder. News televised anywhere else is pure sensationalism.

Between programs come the commercials; they resemble those produced for drive-in movie screens in the late fifties: product containers dancing in circles, puppets laughing too hard, pretty girls cured by herbal pills or sweetened by toothpaste squeezed from the middle of a tube. There are ads for heavy industry, too: sixty-second spots touting drill presses, forklifts, and corrugated doors. I love it all—I'm even saving up to buy one of those big doors.

Rick Wacker and I have been promised our own appearance on TV, just as soon as the new computerized language lab is up and running. The local TV news crew is supposed to be out for the opening. This advanced facility is designed— Professor Zhong keeps telling us—to bolster the instruction of English, but so far neither Wacker nor I have been allowed inside it. We've tried enough times to get a peek, but Professor Zhong always has an excuse: chairs must be ordered, thong sandals for those using the lab have not arrived. It's supposed to be a dust-free environment. Meanwhile the lab door is always locked, the keeper of the key always at lunch. So I'm still waiting for my call to TV stardom.

This afternoon, as we wander through the Administration Building on our own, Wacker swears he is going to catch the key keeper; instead, we make a detour at a makeshift studio on the third floor where a videotape session is in full swing. Several small sets have been constructed, and technicians are wheeling Sony cameras to and fro, lining up a multiple shot of a human heart impaled on a thin steel shaft. It is an instructional film in progress for Anatomy 101.

The director scrutinizes a color monitor where the glistening heart hangs suspended like the Earth against a dark blue background. Meanwhile, a technician has withdrawn a second organ, a pickled brain, from a bucket on the floor. As he sticks it on the spike of another set, he starts chuckling to himself. Then someone else pulls a severed pancreas from the same bucket, scratches his head, and laughs, too. Finally a workman walks in and plops down a second bucket. Everyone crowds around for a look. This bucket contains a whole foot, cleanly sawed off at the ankle. It is the largest foot I've ever seen. As the director reaches in for it, he bursts out laughing, and the whole room is in stitches.

It is an odd sort of omen.

That night Wacker and I are summoned back to the Big Building. The door to the new Language Lab is swung wide open at last, and Professor Zhong waits inside. A crew from the provincial TV network expects to film us here, tomorrow morning, 8:00 A.M. sharp. We'll have two hours to master the equipment.

The lab's impressive: a sparkling facility in white, acoustically baffled, and most likely the single cleanest room in Xi'an with four noisy air-conditioners in the walls. There are forty-eight plexiglass listening booths for our students and a dual master control where Wacker and I can preside simultaneously, cuing up language-learning tapes and dishing out

the latest educational software. There is, however, no software, no language tapes at all to feed this computerized
octopus imported from Norway. All we have is a skimpy
operator's manual left behind by the Norwegian technicians
and the man with the keys to the lab who was trained some
six months ago in English, which the Norwegians barely
spoke and the Chinese technician did not understand. There
are no chairs and no dustless sandals either. We stalk the
room in our socks and hunch over the control console like
home mechanics, more or less puzzled. It should be quite an
entertaining performance.

— : : —

The next day the TV people arrive only an hour late — just in
time, in other words. Our students bring their own chairs
and clean socks. They are ecstatic. It looks like a sock-hop in
a gymnasium of voter booths.

Everyone starts chattering into their microphones and tape
remotes, fiddling with their headphones, grasping switches
and dials. I begin babbling nonsense, truly utter nonsense,
into my master mike and fire up some blank tapes; my
students babble plenty of nonsense back. The camera rolls,
the room overheats, the computer wheezes and hacks. . . .
The whole lab may be virtually useless — in my opinion, a
chalkboard would represent a major breakthrough — but it's
modern, it's technological, it's TV, it is Chinese glitz.

At 7:30 P.M. I appear on regional Chinese TV in a star-
ring role: wise foreigner at the controls of modern high
tech. The footage is a bit raw: black and white, as grainy
as shredded wheat. You can hear it roll on the spool, then

stop in midsentence, stop as if it were whacked off with a meat cleaver.

— : : —

Neither Wacker nor I have trouble handling our celebrity. A clerk at the Binguan says she did see me or Wacker or someone who looked like both of us on TV last night. She pretends to be unimpressed.

After drinking ourselves a little sillier than usual on the rooftop, we pedal home late and spot yet another TV crew filming in a workers' restaurant. We decide to pull up and audition. They let us in. We are given jars of fresh yogurt as we watch them rehearse the cafe scene for a made-for-TV movie. It is the drama of a young couple facing life together in brave new China. One glance and we know the whole storyline.

Wacker inquires: do they need a foreign devil TV star or two as extras? They eye us curiously and say no. They even make us pay for the yogurt. McLuhan be damned. The medium is not the message, just a mirror; it bears the special seal of its culture, and no mere modern invention from communism to television will ever make the slightest rent in the celestial fabric.

We ride back after midnight. Everyone within the Medical College walls is fast asleep. We navigate a few blocks down a pitch-black lane, heave our bikes over the locked iron gate, and climb home.

A week later we make a strange discovery: there's a second Language Lab across the hall from the first. "Maybe a backup," Wacker suggests. "When Lab Number One goes

haywire, who the hell in Xi'an could put it back together
again?"

Good question. Anyway, there it is: absolutely unsullied,
absolutely unused, an exact replica—technological China
looking at itself in a motionless mirror.

ACROSS
A RIVER
OF STARS

I've wrung out my laundry (blue jeans and T-shirts from Hong Kong) until my fingers ache, rinsing the White Cat detergent off in a second metal basin. I hang everything to dry on four wires above my balcony. By noon the whirl-winds, which have peeled off the upper layers of dust from the loesslands, arrive with quiet vehemence. Thick clouds expunge the sky and scrape along the ground. I have to turn on the lights to see inside. Outside, the infantry of tiled roofs has disappeared.

The first great dust storm makes Xi'an a swale of smoky jade. Rototillers with caged pigs in their trailers thump up streets laid on end like ladders, and children in square wooden buggies with built-in potties slide down from the sky. My black bike cartwheels across an intersection, its inner tubes turned inside out and dangling from the axles like intestines.

Then the bare light bulb in my living room begins to swing, yanking its cord out of the wall socket, and with it comes the whole waking and sleeping miscellanea of my life in Xi'an: a canned ham, stir-fried peanuts, and bits of washed cauliflower and cabbage ears; milk still boiling in its wrapper of scum; a white yogurt jar with the Bell Tower emblazoned on its belly, dollops of soft banana-flavored ice cream in a dixie cup, and warm flat breads baked over coal in a cement oven; stale ballpoint pens, congealed watch batteries, a hand-cranked village telephone big as a bowling ball, and the Jell-O I've been hoarding in rice bowls in the fridge; ration coupons for rice and wheat and cooking oil, cold noodles with greens smeared in red-hot sauce, and pancakes fried from straight flour; a black vinyl shoulder bag with a pagoda logo embossed in gold, my rag mop and horsetail broom; pirated textbooks filched from the forbidden second floor of the Foreign Language Bookstore, a splay of black spider bananas, and blobs of desacked quilt spleen; a straw mat, the seeds and grains and shovels and pitchforks city farmers leave in the middle of the street for thrashing; a rewound videotape of *Singin' in the Rain* showing Cyd Charisse's provocative thighs (banned on campus), the entire facade of the Sian Restaurant for Health and Food Curing, and at the end of the cord a popular orange plastic knickknack for sale everywhere—a Mommy Deer With Fawn, aka Bambi in Chains. . . .

Before this dust storm arrived, it had rained forty-nine hours straight and heated up to ninety-nine degrees; now there's no temperature at all and not a single raindrop or bead of sweat. It was never drier anywhere on the face of the earth. Visibility: about a block.

I walk toward the Big Building, shielding my eyes, leaning forward; clumps of students and teachers congeal in the dust, swaying in and out of focus like lost caravans. Lights on every floor of the Big Building glow like paper lanterns suspended from stalactites in a cave as big as the sky. I see Fred and Rita walking home, with Wacker trailing them. As light hits the dust, it is sometimes yellow, sometimes purple, so dispersed and fractured that Fred and Rita and Wacker seem to be sailing toward me on a backlit stage. They are enclosed in pulsing halos, like Buddhas strolling hand in hand through a pulverized ghetto.

— : : —

Class picture day. Outside it is pouring rain and downright chilly. Inside it is just as cold. We pose as a group, my students and I, with Professor Zhong and the President of the Medical College and, for no particular reason, Fred and Rita's teaching assistant. Perhaps she is standing in for Dr. Fu. Fu hasn't show up, although he promised to appear.

We've run the usual gamut. Earlier I went to the Big Building to collect my final month's pay and travel bonus. I sat down at the little table while the clerk went into the cage, then dutifully counted out my bundle of ten-kwai notes. Others, seeking reimbursement from the college for expenses, watched me, nodding and smiling, fans of bus chits between their fingers.

At ten o'clock the rain came down harder. We were supposed to meet outside for the picture, but inside the main lobby everyone was running in different directions and the photography crew was late. No one was in charge. At noon, it somehow comes together, we line up in four loose rows on the main stairway.

I remember the studio at the Xiaozhai market where I posed when I first arrived in Xi'an. My likeness was required for the production of the working papers I carry everywhere in red and white plastic covers. Not a single instant camera system in the city, just a big box camera with plates, an iron-leg tripod, a chattering photographer diving under a black hood. I was surprised they didn't use gun powder and a match. The equipment for our class picture is only a bit more modern; it reminds me of how they took class pictures when I was a child.

Afterwards I take what I think will be my last long ride the familiar way—north from the campus gate, east past the post office, north again past the free market and the Binguan and the traffic circle where a muddy canal crosses—to see the rim of the city wall, not part of this age   a seven-mile dragon of rammed earth. I reach the wall in twenty minutes, as usual, and ride at random for an hour. The air is wet. Hundreds of faces on every street, none familiar. I stop only because my back tire is flat again. Never any trouble locating a repair-man to pump it up and this one refuses to charge me. I thank him and do my little bow, my guttural cackles of appreciation.

Back home, I take my red-flower thermos downstairs to the boiler and, thoughts elsewhere, bang it lightly against the wall; the glass liner shatters inside with a pop and twinkle, a delicate collapse, like letting the air out of a ghost.

Later that evening Mr. Jing stops by to say goodbye. He delivers our class picture, a 6″ × 8″ black-and-white glossy. On the back are the names in English and Chinese of my students as they appear on the other side—seventeen doctors disheveled and dazed, all in starched white shirts, untucked at the waist. Professor Zhong squints on my right; he wears a formal Mao suit. (We learned just this morning that he was officially accepted into the Chinese Communist Party on July the Fourth.) I'm square in the middle of the front row, dressed in the tight blue corduroy sports coat I bought downtown; I'm bearded, balding, emaciated—a White Russian on the run. Rita comes over, takes a peek, and can't stop laughing; it's the worst class picture she's ever seen. "It looks," she says, "like the portrait of a Chinese reformatory."

In bed, later that night, I wonder what they're doing next door in Dr. Fu's apartment. It sounds like remodeling. On the other side of the wall, the screens are shifting, hammers are flying, ladders and scaffolding are walking across the floor like enormous praying mantises. I can't sleep from anticipation. I can feel the end coming now.

In the morning, Dr. Fu announces that he has been transferred to Shanghai. It's as if a new China has finally arrived, even if it's only by its fingertips.

— : : —

Bundled in the vaults of the memory like sticks of incense, every inch of China seems sweet. But in the ruins of Xi'an are all the bitter lessons of oblivion. Once read, they confirm our fate. The gates open on a city of fallen emperors and gods; golden tiles and vermilion towers are heaped low in alleyways, forgotten and mute, emblems of our own journeys into oblivion. Our shadows score the earth until the dark creases fill with level dust; decomposed, we too are rendered wordless by our passage.

Even connecting the present to the past, threading the holy ruins of Xi'an to their restorations afterwards, I can find but one thread of continuity, carved in stone and formed from dust—the continuity of the dead which alone imparts an enduring pattern to this tapestry of destruction. How foolish to think of transcendence or meaning in a city so unrelentingly grim and unromantic.

Yet any journey worth taking is an act of self-excavation; whole regions of what we once were are eroded, exposing the under layers of what we truly are; surely we undertake such journeys into exile in hopes of finding another self, more extensive and intense. Moving in tandem with the dead, what has died within—more than what is born in its place— defines us, and this does not so much negate as sharpen our sense of life.

From the beginning I meant to compose an image of what I found at Xi'an. But I've failed, obviously, in this act of pathetic self-importance; in its stead, I've learned to be insignificant.

I understood nothing at first, least of all myself or why I had come for something I could not identify, or even imagine. After thirty-five years of comfort, to chuck everything in on no more than a whim and cross the dateline, was an act beyond reason. Never had I been more lonely, more miserable, more lost, and never will I come closer to a real kind of ecstasy, an elemental one, the kind that can only come when there is nothing. The old staleness, coiled within me, crumbled day by day.

I've come back now with fewer illusions, particularly about the self and what it might be.

In the long view the fate of each element is oblivion; there are no exceptions. Even religions must die. It's perfectly obvious in Xi'an, where religion itself is in ruins: there's no mystery about its fate. Or about our own. Whether the self is a searing wind or a deep well, the end is the same. One burns, the other drowns.

Yet Xi'an is more than the perfect city of the dead: it is also the mirror of the heavens. For thirty centuries it has resisted final ruin. Once you learn how to see in the dark, the old capital becomes as wide and deep as the Milky Way. You wade knee-deep in dust across a river of stars.

WHITE RABBIT

We set out in the morning for Hua Shan, one of the five sacred peaks of China. Hua Shan is a cluster of five sharp summits, the Fingertips of the Immortals, part of a sudden wall at the eastern end of the plains of Xi'an where the Wei meets the Yellow River and the Yellow River bends east to the sea.

There are so few accounts of Hua Shan in the West that we wonder if an outsider has ever climbed it. Over the centuries monks carved stairs by hand up stone monoliths to the top, otherwise inaccessible; but we have been assured that this stairway to heaven ends in the courtyard of a monastery where guests, even four foreign guests, can spend the night. We've laid our plans accordingly, although our plans are truly pointless. We will merely climb, climb with the rest, and see where the path takes us.

The Friday afternoon train from Xi'an was a milk run and

it was three hours before we even reached the Hua Shan Station, just sixty miles east. We were armed with the necessary permits, provided by our work unit and otherwise difficult to obtain. On the way we saw a long chain of earthen villages and green rapeseed fields where peasants had festooned the graves of their ancestors with wheels of fall flowers. Then the high, bare desert plateau ended abruptly.

We walked down a vacant street from the station, inquired about a hotel, and turned right along the main county road. It was a mile from the village of Hua Yin where we saw the bare dome of the sacred mountain for the first time, 8000 feet straight up over the rim of a deep canyon—like a vision in a Chinese landscape, remote, wild, a painted scroll returned to stone, to its origins.

We talked our way into a Chinese hotel located at the main intersection of the village. Our room was spartan: four cots with bean mattresses and cotton quilts, a washstand with four basins, two thermoses of boiled water, a single cuspidor, and a view from the second story of the brick latrine out back. Fifty cents a person. The village was more alluring. At dusk we walked up the main avenue lined with food and souvenir stands for a solid mile, crowds thick the whole way, but no other foreigners about.

The noise in the street continued well after midnight, and our sleep was broken countless times after that by trucks crossing the main intersection, drivers laying into horns with unrelenting bravado. By 6:00 A.M. we gave up fighting for rest, sat up in unison, smiled at each other, shrugged, and packed for the trek.

— : : —

At dawn the stalls are still open. No one in Hua Yin ever seems to sleep. At the end of the street, we come upon a road show, a traveling carnival—with banners portraying bears riding motorcycles—under a little big top pitched beside the old temple. Through this pavilion, up two flights of stairs, is the gate to Hua Shan. The ticket taker examines our permits and turns us back. An official takes us down to another hotel, and after an hour of haggling issues us a second set of passes for which we are forced to pay an additional fee. Bureaucratic banditry, we complain, and everyone nods.

Tickets in hand, we cross through the entry gates and are twice swallowed: first by the throngs of Chinese making an early start on this narrow trail of loose rock and gravel, then by the mammoth walls of the Luo River Canyon. It is twelve miles to the top of the white dome, to the Peak of the Immortals, but from the bottom it looks a thousand miles away, a thousand miles up.

Across the river the vertical canyon walls, engraved in fine calligraphy, are honeycombed with the footholds of Taoist hermits, chiseled to reach their private perches. A mile into the canyon we see the first of the ruined shrines. Somehow the Red Guards hauled their hammers even here; the remains have the imprint of human rather than natural dissolution. Then the path levels out on a wide, green pasture and snakes through walled gardens. We rest at the doorstep of three stone huts. A monk steps out and invites us back to look at his shrine, a cave dug out at the base of the cliff. The altar inside is dark and musty, sagging under the weight of canned food and half-burned incense sticks.

At every turn peasants have set up shop, hawking noodles, tea, steamed breads, ice lollies, and good-luck charms snipped from tin. I buy a brightly painted charm in the shape of a bat and wear it around my neck. Some sellers have pitched awnings — sheets propped up on sticks — to block the sun; most simply have cast their wares on the ground. At every vista, itinerant photographers produce hastily developed negatives for those without cameras; customers are obliged to carry these images in long ribbons up and down the mountain. The most sought-after trailside photographers rely on shameless props, posing their subjects in the saddle of a stallion with swirling mane and flaring nostrils, plywood cut-outs drenched in gold, white, and vermilion paints. To supply vendors and the guesthouses farther up, peasants ferry crates of rice, vegetables, cola, and beer suspended from the ends of poles. These are heavy loads to shoulder up steep, sliding, irregular terrain in the warmth of the sun, where I repeatedly twist my ankles on the loose rocks. Moreover, the passage becomes narrower and the crowds slower the farther we walk, and once, for nearly an hour, we are unable to pass one porter carrying a thick, wide door on his back.

The Chinese do not go into nature alone. This high country trek resembles a Sunday outing in Shanghai. Everyone, from infants dressed in pink and red to great-great-grandmothers in black, quilted coats, is jammed chest to back, shoulder to shoulder. Monks march beside young soldiers of the People's Liberation Army, and barefoot peasants mingle with the most modern of China's ladies who brave the slopes in Leatherette high heels.

But the most marvelous travelers of all are the old, old women everywhere. They forge ahead on canes or sticks torn from the hillsides and stripped clean. They are slowed only by their bound feet, the tiny feet of infants, the once-erotic deformations of a practice not legal in China since 1911. They travel in determined clusters, never yielding to shoves from behind, and they answer the complaints of impatient youth with sharp retorts fired in the harsh dialect of Shaanxi Province. We encounter them at every switchback where they have pulled off to rest in the sparse shade. Sometimes they waylay us with a smile or gesture, then turn away with a gruff laugh of utter astonishment. We are impossible figures in their universe, probably the first foreign devils they've ever run across. One old woman who engages us in conversation can't stop laughing. It is the first day of fall by our reckoning, but here, on the older calendar of the East, it is a Taoist holiday, and these short women in black, with prayer beads, medals, and flowers pinned to their collars, are pilgrims of an earlier age for whom Mao and Deng are perhaps no more than names from another village beyond these mountains. As girls they first climbed these mountains when all the shrines were whole and the hermits fought for a cave in the canyon cliffs. They are now willing to crawl to the summit on their knees if that's what it takes. They have allowed two days to reach the top, content to spend a night asleep on the hard trailside.

By noon we are above the canyon wall, in a realm of pure stone, of vertical shafts. The journey will be steeper ahead.

We rest at a spring surging through a pile of boulders and soak our arms and foreheads. The sky is cloudless. We have left the shade in the canyon below and are gaining altitude quickly, winding through tall shanks and outcroppings.

We come out on the ledge of an abandoned temple. I draw back from the edge. Below: the fold of the canyon, like a crumpled ribbon. Ahead: the Thousand Stairs, a vertical ladder cut into a chimney of rock. The treads are no more than four inches deep, ideal perhaps for bound feet. We must climb in single file on the tips of our toes. To keep from falling backwards into the chasm, we clutch a handrail of chain links anchored by iron pinions. Some are trying to wiggle ahead, to pass whenever an opening appears, even on these vertical stairs. As we near the top, there is a scream behind us. Something falls from the sky. Everyone freezes to the chain. A porter has lost his load; a door screams down the Thousand Stairs like a war kite. When I look back down over my shoulder, I'm eaten by terror; the perspective is too deep to make any sense. But the porter, cursing his misfortune, scrambles back down easily, somehow weaseling through the thicket of clinging bodies. No one was hit or dislodged by what he has dropped—a miracle, in my view. Every year a few dozen people fall to their deaths from Hua Shan.

We stop for lunch on the south peak above the Thousand Stairs. Known as the Peak Where Wild Geese Land (Luo Yan Feng), it is the natural equivalent of the Big Wild Goose Pagoda in Xi'an. The only birds we see are thrushes in the thick, red brush of the ravines. No temples are left on the south peak—only a foundation, walls razed to the ground on four sides—where we sit and eat.

The Dark Green Dragon's Spine, a natural bridge resembling the web between thumb and forefinger, connects the southern peak to the other four; we have to cross it next. On either side the drop is long and straight, certainly fatal, and the carved stairs remind me of slats in a suspension bridge. Yet after the Thousand Stairs, the Dragon's Spine is child's play. Once across, the path forks, forming a loop around the great summits.

We walk two miles east, scramble up an unmarked hillside, and reach a Taoist monastery on the western peak while the sun is still high. The temple courtyard is very nearly a cul-de-sac, but a set of stairs in one corner serves as a ladder. We climb above the tiled roofs and come out on top of the dome we sighted from Hua Yin yesterday.

Nothing is before us but a sea of thin, fragrant air, the crease of a river, a plain of dust. A few pine trees hook out from fissures in the mile-long cliff under our feet. The Peak of the Immortals, it embodies their perspective. We lean back on a thin ledge facing southwest, stretch out, and talk for the rest of the afternoon, mostly about America, which has taken on its own exaggerated, unreal shape in our absence. Below, all of ground-zero China is blanketed in the haze of postliberation coal plants and heavy industry. By dusk, it disappears, fading out, and we can only see the surrounding mountain ranges, layered one after the other in endless screens, golden in the setting sun, then blue and charcoal under a wheel of stars.

The monastery, too, comes alive in the darkness. Pilgrims continue to arrive: the old, old women—seated on the steps, burning fake paper money, stirring the ashes, praising their favorite god—are discussing the exchange rates of heaven. . . . In the prayer hall many travelers bed down in tiered bunks rising up two walls. The altar is dense with offerings. The monks toss strings of firecrackers onto the paving stones, chasing away any ghosts who might have accompanied us up the Dragon's Spine.

We secure two bare rooms, monks' quarters, on the second floor opposite the prayer hall. Sunburnt and sore, I fall asleep at once on the bare boards of my stall.

— : : —

Hua Shan is laden with dreams. The very shape of its outcroppings are the structure of legend and art. Emperor Han Wu, founder of the Ming dynasty, dreamed his whole life of making the pilgrimage to Hua Shan. In his visions, he was always led to the Peak of the Immortals by a white rabbit. When in his old age he finally made the trek, he found no discrepancy between reality and vision; the inner and outer worlds had reached their spontaneous harmony.

— : : —

The Great Shithouse of Hua Shan is a crude shack cantilevered over the edge of a cliff, located to one side of the monastery. This toilet at the sacred summit in the center of China must rank among the top ten most precarious privies in the world. Its wooden floorboards are rotten; the bowls are nothing but wide open holes. Below, on the chin of a cliff, monks gather the excrement in buckets at dawn and carry it to their herb gardens. It's the middle of the night. I can see stars through the walls. I turn off the flashlight and stagger back up to bed.

— : : —

Descending on Sunday, we run into a traffic jam at the top of the Thousand Stairs. So many are coming up the mountain that we must wait on the unshaded path three hours for our turn. Everyone's angry. There's an eruption of tempers and shoves, until some PLA soldiers arrive to settle matters. When our turn comes, we find our heels less flexible than our toes on the shallow treads. Some go down sideways, others prefer a backwards approach, and the old women, wisest of all, descend the stairs sitting down, taking each step on their rumps. I do the same.

Once beneath the canyon rim, we find a few strands of shade. I'm surprised by what I hadn't noticed on the way up—the steepness of the path, even in its lower reaches, the lushness of the thickets and flowers, and the large number of children, dressed so that they seem like a chain of flowers, hiking up with parents and grandparents.

We do not reach the gate until the sun sets, sets in our eyes so we can't see ahead. Parched, we buy drinks in the street and sit down on benches under a pavilion roof and lick our wounds—twisted ankles, stiffened thighs. The open pavilion is inundated with pilgrims. They unroll straw mats and lie down to sleep. Young couples wander to and fro, rented flashlights in their fists, waiting for the moon to rise. They have come to climb Hua Shan at night, at its most dangerous.

Once I rise and follow Wacker through the streets of the village—the night market crowded and noisy—and by sheer accident I catch the elbow of a peasant woman with a ladle of boiling water. My chest is scalded, yet no burn appears. I think of how Fred has managed to climb the Thousand Stairs of Hua Shan despite his fear of heights, a fear I also share, the fear of peering down from these pinnacles.

— : : —

We are sitting in a temple under a sacred mountain. It is perfect. I believe that one should count one's life blessed if there are seven perfect days in its span, a week scattered through memory where every second is an ineradicable source of light. At Hua Shan, I float into just such an eddy on a quicksilver river that might have flowed through the valleys of the moon, so remote is it from the familiar gray stream-beds of the earth. I sit like a rock in the courtyard of this temple, where sacrifices had been made to the 36,000 gods for centuries, and hold each lovely detail of the day as tightly as I had each link in the chain on the Thousand Stairs, not wanting to let go of the landscape or of the people, from the bound-footed pilgrims to my countrymen who would soon be dispersed across the world, whom I might never see again. I wait under a white dome of stairs carved to the stars, powerless to hold any of this for long, and feel myself crumble; I am swept into the sad flow, every bone in my body asleep and dreaming. Abruptly a sirocco rises from the plains of Xi'an, uncoiling like a warm spirit out of the west. It is autumn in northern China and the ice has begun to form, but under the western mountain it is summer at midnight. The moon rises full and shining over the peak, its light passing through a gate of green jade.

IV. STONE

THE QUEEN IN KUNMING

I returned to China after an absence of several years, eager to reach Xi'an and see what changes had overtaken the old capital, but I traveled slowly, stopping in remote Kunming where I was delayed for a week.

The changes were obvious wherever I went. My domestic flight from Guilin to Kunming, for example, was aboard a well-appointed, modern jet, the first I had encountered inside China. The seats, even the seatbelts, of that Boeing 737 clone were unbroken; the air supply cones shone above our heads like stars. But my fellow passengers, bound for home, had not advanced at breakneck speed into the new Age of High Technology. Perhaps none had ever flown on a jet. They boarded the plane as they would a city bus, shoving every step of the way, across the airstrip, up the stairs, and into their assigned seats. I pushed as hard as they did. Once seated, the pace accelerated. Overwhelmed by the smooth plastic and vinyl splendors of the cabin, my fellow passengers could not keep their hands off the reading lamp switches or air nozzles, their arms and fingers rifling in every direction like a signal corps gone berserk. Not even the stewardess could restore order. Twice she sprinted down the aisle, chiding stragglers to strap in, but few of them had ever buckled a seatbelt and they ignored her. As the jet lifted from the runway, screaming low over the karst peaks of Guilin, I heard a chorus of gleeful awe ripple up and down the rows.

The man next to me wore a faded green workers' jacket, hard black shoes with raised heels (high fashion in China), and red silk long underwear (despite the temperate climate of the southwest). He rolled up his sleeve, displaying two silver, spring-wound Chinese Seagull watches on his wrist, smiled provocatively, then leaned across and minutely examined my $4.95 black-plastic quartz timepiece. Later he withdrew the bag from the pocket of the seat in front and used it the same way as the other passengers: to clear his throat. Thus was the vomit bag of the West transformed into the disposable spittoon of the East. China has been renowned for centuries for incessant hawking and spitting; oddly enough, however, in a country without a surgeon general's report, where heavy-puffer Deng Xiao Ping speaks of the Seven Virtues of the Cigarette, no one smoked on the flight to Kunming. It was the only smoke-free chamber I had sat in since returning to China.

We landed on schedule—also a first for me—and walked across the unlit tarmac for half a mile under a light rain. The airfield at Kunming is where American pilots formed the Flying Tigers in 1940 to assist in the battle against Japan;

where the U.S. Fourteenth Air Force resided throughout World War II; where each night during the long war of occupation the Chinese filled in the craters of the latest bombing raid by hand. Now there's not a trace of an American presence. Here history is swallowed up overnight.

My taxi, which also transported an open bucket of gasoline in the front seat, followed an unpaved back road into the heart of the city, depositing me at the gate of the Kunming Hotel. I entered the lobby in a state of dread. In the weeks before, in Canton and Guilin—both cities more familiar with foreign travelers—the hotel staff had been incompetent, uncaring, even savage. Chinese television was still broadcasting a series that summarized the situation with its ominous title: "*Civilized* Hotel Service." Luckily, the Kunming Hotel was a bit more advanced. It's true that my toilet broke the first night, but when I fetched the floor attendant, who was napping in a chair beside the water boiler where the room thermoses were filled, she fixed the plumbing immediately.

Kunming, just 200 miles from Vietnam, on a high, lush plateau in extreme southwest China, is famed for its gardens and herbs. It is equally well-known as the center of the largest concentration of minorities in China—some six million members of several dozen ethnic groups. The minority influence is strong, imparting a diversity and relaxed pace of life—even a few flashes of color—otherwise absent in modern Chinese cities where the racially homogeneous Han make up 99 and 44/100s percent of the population. Kunming is even less sophisticated than Xi'an, a quality I immediately admired. The only problem was the Queen—Queen Elizabeth II of England.

The Queen was on her first visit to China and for some reason Kunming was part of her itinerary. No one at the hotel knew when she was due to arrive; even worse, no one knew where she and the press were to stay. There were signs, however. Ominous signs. The hotel staff received new uniforms the day after I arrived. The uniforms were stiff, formal Western hotel attire, down to the immaculate white gloves, which the workers wore with arrogance. Groundkeepers were suddenly marshalling vases of flowers into position in front of the main entrance. In the afternoon, I watched as the staff placed potted plants on exquisite dinner plates, plates rinsed off in the parking lot fountain where the taxi drivers washed their cars faithfully twice a day.

Heralded as the Kingdom of Flowers, celebrated for its luxuriant horticulture, renowned for its vast botanical pharmacopoeia, Kunming was nevertheless bursting with more camellia and rose blooms than usual for October. Pennants were mounted on all the prominent buildings, and blank banners were stretched across Dongfeng Dong Lu, the main avenue. I would discover that these wordless banners had been strung over every block where the Queen's limousine was scheduled to pass in Kunming, a bannering of many miles in every direction. A block from the Kunming Hotel the entire sidewalk had been transformed into a bower of paper lanterns, illuminated by electric bulbs. The locals took their children there every evening and lifted them up to view the faces of birds and animals painted on the lanterns. All the while, the young staff of the Kunming Hotel kept up a running ruse with the foreign guests to the effect that the flowers, banners, pennants, and lanterns, as well as their new uniforms, caps, and gloves, were nothing out of the ordinary.

Then the same friendly staff began to kick out the guests, nearly all of whom had paid premium prices for accommodations as part of their expensive China tours. The staff started up Tuesday morning and finished up the next day. The luckier tour groups somehow found a flight out of Kunming or a floor in a Chinese hotel, but I had seen some of the lesser hotels and decided to concoct a ruse of my own. I wrote a message, in English, introducing myself to the manager. I could not locate the manager, although he had a desk, prominently displayed in a corner of the lobby, with two telephones and a placard turned toward onlookers which read "Manager on Duty" to explain his absence. I walked the length of that long lobby twice, deposited my message on the Manager's desk, and retired to my seventh floor room. Half an hour later I was startled when my wastebasket began to ring—that was where, when clearing the desk, I had stationed the telephone. I was summoned to appear immediately in the offices of Mr. Nian Jia Fu, Manager of the Kunming Hotel.

There I was seated with some ceremony upon a sofa. A translator, Ms. Zhang, joined us, as did a chef and several underlings who served tea and a variety of fine Yunnan pastries and breads. In an instant, I was elevated from commoner to Number One Guest. Mr. Nian and I hit it off at once. He invited me to an intimate banquet in one of the hotel's many dining rooms, where we sampled the regional cuisine: Ji Zong mushrooms—long, stringy, and outrageously expensive, favored by the Japanese for their ginseng-like properties; sweet ham and fried goat cheese, which make Kunming the capital of Chinese fast food; and Across-the-Bridge Noodles, a hearty dip-it-yourself fondue. Every dish was laden with miraculous, healthful, fat-reducing herbs and spices. Mr. Nian took me for the advance guard of the Western media who arrived ahead of the Queen, destined to make Kunming famous.

Thereafter, I would carry the business card of Nian Jia Fu throughout Kunming, wielding it much as Marco Polo had the seal of an earlier Mongol emperor on his travels. Even so, there would be many gates I could not pass through. The Queen's visit set up lofty obstacles and ever higher ranks would come into play, hindering my simplest movements.

Nevertheless, I came to realize that the most restricted of all visitors to Kunming was the Queen herself. She could not move in any direction without the walls of history collapsing upon her. Those walls had become her armor which, turn as she might, she could never shed. In short, she was doomed to spectacle.

— : : —

For all his string-pulling, the manager could not arrange a flight to Xi'an for a full week. The Queen was not due for a few days. I was very nearly the sole guest of the towering Kunming Hotel, which lay in wait, ravenous, for the full Western press to arrive. In the interim, Mr. Nian suggested that I book a car and stay overnight in the Stone Forest (Shi Lin) at a sister guest house to the east, returning, well-rested, to greet the Royal Party.

An hour out of Kunming my driver stops at what he calls

the Nut House on the shores of Lake Yangzhong. The Nut House is a stately prerevolutionary building that reminds me of both a train station and an inn. I am served a glass of tea and fresh walnuts in the shell. Stepping outside, I can see farmers driving oxen across the terraces above the lake. This spot is where the American Air Force partook of R&R during World War II. You wouldn't know it if you hadn't served here in the forties. Today, there's no indication anything ever happened. The earth itself seems to erase the occurrences of the day. The Yunnan plateau possesses only the elemental colors: the red of the soil, the green of the hillsides, the white of limestone, the blue of the sky; a palette serene yet wild, at times unnerving.

There's not a single billboard out here. Neon is nonexistent. The villages are formed of clay. Long red peppers and yellow ears of corn dangle from trees and hang from tiled roofs or on walls, curing in the autumn sunlight. Along the highway we pass horses, carts, and herds of goats. The shoulders of the road are coated with rice, spread out to dry and to be sorted. The round kilns of brickmakers are clustered along the banks of wide rivers, one after another like the tents of nomadic tribes.

At the end of the road, a four hour drive from Kunming, the Stone Forest rises as from a geologist's pipe dream: acres of vertical limestone shafts exposed 270 million years ago when the ocean receded from southwest China. Rain and wind have drilled creases and fissures. It's like a cavern raised entirely above ground, its dome lopped off by the eons and opened to clear sky.

I unpack in a room at the Shi Lin Guest House and arrange

to meet Mr. Lin, my driver, the next day. It's late afternoon and most of the daytrippers are on buses back to Kunming. I head for the entrance to the Stone Forest as two camels are led away by photographers-for-hire. I seem to have the park to myself. Several miles of pathways curl through the karst pinnacles and branch off, skirting reflecting pools, then rising on stone steps to pavilions pitched on limestone summits. The Chinese, as always, have named the more fanciful formations for what they might resemble: Mother and Child, Phoenix Combing Its Wings, Camel Riding An Elephant, Rhinoceros Gazing At The Moon. I'm without a map and the farther I go, the more lost I become. At twilight, a forest of stone becomes stiller than one of living trees, emptier and colder. Fortunately, I come across three Chinese sightseers and follow them, but they lead me into a cul-de-sac. We all scratch our heads and go separate ways. Purely by persistence, I find a way out of the maze.

My room is more than one might reasonably hope for at this far end of the world. The mosquito net draped over my narrow bed has been ripped open. In the bathroom, the tub is on a high pedestal; the Victory-brand toilet is near defeat. The front door is so crooked in its frame that anything could slip through its cracks, from rat to cat. The television is decorative; it receives no stations whatsoever. Outside, the Stone Forest sleeps. The air is fragrant; the sky is choked with stars.

Completely rested, I cross a bridge into a Yi minority village at dawn. The houses and little stores are made of red earth. The roofs are gray-tiled. The Yi farmers are working the fields in their traditional clothing—bright reds and golds.

The old women haunt the roads and Guest House gates, hawking embroidered wares with the tenacity of aluminum siding salesmen. I elude them only after I find my driver warming up his Russian Bear sedan. We cross the red and white, green and blue frontier back to Kunming.

When I approach the reception desk, the clerk, whom I remember clearly from two day's past, brushes me off. There are no rooms. I present the manager's card. He stares at it and marvels. How did you get this card, he asks; he's frankly amazed. Eventually I get my room.

— : : —

Although China provided England with its first cup of tea in the seventeenth century, no reigning British sovereign had set foot on Chinese soil until Queen Elizabeth arrived. Her government had just signed an agreement to return Hong Kong, the last great Crown Colony of the East, to China in 1997. It therefore surprised many, and dismayed not a few, that the receptions staged for the Queen, first in Beijing, then in Shanghai, were rather cool. Longtime observers remarked that the Queen, whose normal expression was as dour as her hats were dowdy, was smiling even less than usual on her "historic and unprecedented visit" to the Middle Kingdom.

On the Queen's fifth day in China, however, as the Royal Delegation trundled southward to Kunming, Her Majesty's reception warmed considerably. She was treated to a magnificent welcome. For several miles, from the airport to the gates of the Provincial Guest House, the people of Kunming lined the streets ten and twelve deep. They stood on the wide boulevards all morning and most of the afternoon in order to provide a few seconds of applause as the Queen's motorcade of old black limousines hurtled by. Later, a portion of this measureless throng ringed the Queen in the Guest House, maintaining a vigil of smiles well into the night.

The Queen's spokesman, Michael Shea, a gentleman distinguished enough in appearance and manner to play this role in the movies, rhapsodized upon the outpouring of adoration in Kunming. It was the first genuinely grand news he could report that week, and Mr. Shea was especially expansive when he came to estimate the size of the crowds — at least half a million, he said, a figure he later raised to seven hundred thousand. The press had no way to challenge his estimates, since they had arrived on a separate plane and traveled from the airport in a different caravan, fifteen minutes behind the Queen.

At fifteen minutes behind the Queen (that is, at fifteen minutes behind history), Kunming might after all have remade itself and looked to these reporters like any other Chinese city: dreadful, colorless, full of people. But Kunming was not like any other Chinese city, Mr. Shea now declared, because it had sensed the singular importance of this historic moment and responded with the largest single reception ever accorded Queen Elizabeth II. It was, in fact, the largest overseas reception ever witnessed by any British monarch in history.

The press, however, had not come to Kunming gunning for stories about the "extraordinary" reception or the "historic" nature of the Royal Visit to China (to use the adjectives that Mr. Shea kept springing like clay pigeons); thus, no one bothered to take a pot shot at the spokesman's tallies. Instead, the press was shooting for real headlines: not statistics, but scandals. Such a scandal had unfolded that morning, before the planes left for Kunming. Prince Philip, Duke of Edinburgh, husband to the Queen, had insulted the Chinese. What the Duke had said was what the press wanted repeated, but the Queen's man kept talking about the crowds in the streets.

Both parties were merely the world looking from the outside in. Inside was China, not needing to look back out, taking in the Queen and the press and the few stray foreigners like myself who happened to be in Kunming at that moment. Neither receptions nor scandals were the story; the way we were all taken in was the story. Thus, in a crazed way, the Queen's visit *was* a historic moment, if a historic moment is an occasion upon which all of a culture's peculiar resources are required to attend. In China, these resources are peculiar indeed.

So is history. Only at the center of events, where the Queen and the press must stand and from which an account of history is usually broadcast to the world, does everything seem ordinary and logical, because in China one is always kept in the dark, and the machinery of the occasion shifts silently past, undetected.

As an accidental member of the "unprecedented" crowd, I could not tell how many people were actually in the street on the afternoon and I had no inside information about how big a scandal was being covered up by Mr. Shea. I could, however, answer a more fundamental question: namely, why so many Chinese came out to welcome the Queen. The answer was that the Chinese were standing on the side of the street out of boredom and curiosity, to do something rather than nothing, to see what new thing might pass through their streets. They were as innocent of diplomacy and politics as children let out of school to see a parade. While some cadres and party chiefs were undoubtedly pressured to bolster the reception and swell the ranks, the people needed little prodding to participate, even if it meant standing around empty-handed most of the day.

The reception was a false not in the sense that it was orchestrated, which (haphazardly) it was; and not false in the sense that people were conscripted and forcibly positioned in ranks along the Queen's parade route, which they surely were not. The pageant was false in the stranger sense that virtually none of the spectators had the slightest notion who Queen Elizabeth was or where Her Majesty reigned. England might as well have been Java or Peru.

On the morning of her arrival, half of Kunming seemed to be milling in the square, at the center of the city, strutting up and down in their finery, more interested in using their new cameras on each other than on anything so abstract as the Queen. It was not until I was on the square a full hour that I understood what had happened. Most of the one million workers had simply been given an unexpected day off.

Watching the peasants, factory workers, educators, bureaucrats and the minorities in costume, many with their families, strolling aimlessly through the square, I understood why they were throwing themselves headlong into the day's event, although the event itself made no sense. This was a party, a big party; only the streets of the city were big enough to hold it. Flowers were stacked in wide pots at every intersection along the Queen's way, and the people were delighted to stand by and enjoy them. Directly across the main boulevard from the square, huge red balloons swayed on hemp tethers high above a slanting bank of roses. The children were thrilled by the sight. The rose beds, a full block long, had been trimmed and sculpted to spell out "Welcome" in English. People kept walking the block, back and forth, enjoying the landscaping. Only I seemed impatient. I kept looking at my watch, frustrated by not knowing when to expect the Queen. Everyone else went about the day with no such concern.

As it turned out, it was almost nightfall by the time the Queen's entourage arrived. I had returned by then to the Kunming Hotel. The sidewalks were full. I climbed to the top of the hotel wall, where I could look over the crowd into the street. The street was empty of buses and bicycles, carts and animals. The police controlled the crowds first by allowing them to swell into the street, then by beating them back to the sidewalk until they were compressed like sheaves of wheat.

We all waited a long time. Once we heard a vehicle approaching, but it proved to be a water truck again, the same old street-cleaner that had been working since noon to keep the dust down for the Queen. We cheered its appearance and laughed, laughed perhaps at ourselves, because it was not for us that the dust was wetted down. Suddenly an older couple—Westerners from a tour group—left the sidewalk and strutted out into the street, taking a bow: the stand-in King and Queen. We applauded and laughed again.

Finally there was the silence, just a moment's worth, when

we all sensed the cars were about to appear. Then we were all disappointed. The first limousine featured a Chinese official hanging half out of the passenger's window, clapping his hands together like two gongs and nodding to the crowd. This was the Ed McMahon of Kunming, priming the applause meter. We clapped, murmured in unison, surged forward for a view. I never determined which car held the Queen, although I believe that I did glimpse her hat, and I am certain that I beheld her hand extended partly out the second or third limousine window, waving indefinitely.

The crowd dispersed. None of the cars had stopped at the Kunming Hotel, but when I walked through the courtyard to the lobby entrance, I found much of the staff outside, lined up to form a funnel. A few minutes later the reporters began to pull up in beaten taxis and bashed Nissan minivans. They were tired, most of them, metallic suitcases of equipment in hand. The staff clapped in unison as the media straggled in. I was standing by a reporter from Beijing who snickered; Kunming was as provincial as ever, he said: here, hotel workers even clapped for the press.

Ten minutes after the press filed in, a taxi pulled up with a red carpet in its trunk. Later I saw the carpet beside an elevator, stored like a massive jelly roll. Intended for the press, it had arrived just a little late, and was ignored for days afterwards.

— : : —

Late that night, on the second floor of the Kunming Hotel, in a special hall fitted for the occasion as an auditorium, spokesman Michael Shea was still dodging questions, but finally he relented. He began to smooth over the most recent dents in the royal armor.

"It's a well-known physiological fact," he proclaimed, "that people in different parts of the world have eyes that are differently shaped. My eyes are round."

No reporter disputed his pronouncement, which makes sense only when placed in the context of the aforementioned scandal. This morning in Xi'an, the Queen paid an obligatory call upon Emperor Qin's terra-cotta warriors and steeds. She would have emerged unscathed in warm Kunming tonight, surrounded by hundreds of thousands of false fans, had her husband not engaged some British students at Xi'an in conversation. Poor Prince Philip. He asked the students how long they had been studying in China. They answered six weeks. "If you stay here much longer," the Prince warned, "you will go back with slitty eyes." Adding insult to this injury, Prince Philip also remarked to the students that Beijing had been "ghastly."

Now Mr. Shea is picking up the pieces. He insists that Prince Philip has always been "keen" on China. He remains "keen" this moment. He is "keen" on Beijing, on Shanghai, on Xi'an, and certainly on Kunming. The reporters assembled are tired and bored; they are not revived by the prospect of telexing to their editors on the other side of the world such Milquetoast leads as Kunming: City of Eternal Spring, or Queen Treated Like Royalty, or Prince Really Keen on China. Within 48 hours *The Daily Mail* will ask, Does Britain Need a Terra-cotta Duke? and *The Sun* of London will run an altered picture of Prince Philip's face with the caption, Philip Gets It All Wong. Papers in China, of course, will report nothing of the incident.

The first two minutes I am in the pressroom, within earshot of the bar, I am reminded that the press lives for scandal. Nevertheless, they are here to waste time tracking the minute, monotonous, tedious movements of the Queen in China. They are moving in the wrong direction, toward the apparent center of gravity, not knowing that in China, at least, one has to escape gravity altogether. The Queen in Kunming becomes an interesting story only as one tries to escape her presence. When one retreats to the streets, when one stares into the looking glass which is China at the elaborate processes designed to press the fabric of official reception smooth, then one begins to learn something serious. This culture is a dark star, a furnace for the manufacture of antimatter. However much Chinese officials seem to mismanage and misunderstand, China always triumphs. Everything it takes in is emptied and absorbed.

I am making these grand generalities while watching Mr. Nian Jia Fu slide unobtrusively through the ranks of the international press. He pauses to snap a photo here and there with a cheap instamatic camera. Short, middle-aged, informally dressed, Mr. Nian is not nearly as imposing a figure as Mr. Shea, although he exerts about a thousand times more power here. He takes pictures because this is his pressroom, finished in the finest wood panels and local marble, festooned now with men and women from around the world. The press can not appreciate how dazzling this room is in Kunming. Mr. Nian looks like a nobody.

Sitting at a table in the back, I grab a copy of tomorrow's Royal Itinerary. I've never attended a press briefing before; I'm here under false pretenses, but at this moment I am convinced that an entire segment of the universe from Kunming to Edinburgh is operating under false pretenses.

The Kunming Hotel is certainly in specious overdrive. In each of its rooms the press will discover a bowl of fruit, a shan bag, a letter of welcome, and two new tea cups. Waitresses will wait tables in the dining halls outfitted in bright minority costumes, as though color and smiles were everyday occurrences. Even the hallways are specially doused with perfumes. All this has come after the regular tourists were booted out.

I was the first to wander into the pressroom this evening, where I sat down and ordered a large Tsing Tao beer, but a retired couple from Montana quickly joined me. They were not journalists, either, nor were they a longtime couple. Somewhere between Shanghai and Kunming, they had fallen into a shipboard romance. Each had paid a premium for their China tour, about $4,000, and they and 47 other Americans in their group, kicked out of the Kunming Hotel at 8:30 A.M., resided on the fifth floor of the nearby Camellia Hotel. I happened to know the inside of the Camellia. The elevator did not work. I ask how they like their fifth floor walkup. The man from Montana laughs. "To flush the toilet," he says, "we have to fill it with a hose from the bathtub." She adds: "The bathroom floor has never been scrubbed, not once since the day it was built. I don't understand why."

They are cursing neither the Camellia nor the Kunming Hotel; they've been warned to expect this in China. They seem thrilled. It's an adventure. They're sorry for the Queen. She'll never be turned out of a hotel as long as she lives, nor will she ever get to flush her toilet from the tub. The Queen never has a vacation, they say. She's Queen twenty-four hours a day, every day of the week, whether she likes it or not. She doesn't even get weekends off.

After the press conference, while the Queen eats under the scrutiny of her hosts at her fifth state banquet, I walk up a side street to a local restaurant I spotted yesterday. It is packed on one side with a tour group and on the other side, the noisy side, with Chinese. The staff refuses to seat me on either side. I'm not with a group and I'm not Chinese; therefore, I cannot eat. I end up at a more hospitable, less clean, far cheaper, workers' restaurant, the Olympic Bar and Grill. It once possessed an opulent interior. Now its bright plastic and glass are glazed in cigarette smoke. The fried goat cheese and potatoes are especially good, and together with the Yunnan ham and several other dishes cost less than the can of cola I order. My fellow diners are making workman's banquets of ten and even twenty dishes, of fish and fowl with eyes intact. After each dish they sweep the bones onto the floor, draining bulk beer from bowls. This is not the sort of restaurant, however full of character, night soil and stains of slain duck and pig and odors of coal fire, to which you invite the Queen to tea.

— : : —

Early the next morning, as the Queen partakes of breakfast somewhere behind the high pink walls of Zhenzhuan Villa and the press files out of the Kunming Hill to follow Her

Majesty on her appointed rounds, I walk to the cable office, where, after an hour's delay, I fire off a telegram to Xi'an announcing my imminent arrival. The worker in charge of the foreign section insists upon translating my telegram text back into English after I arranged for the Assistant Hotel Manager to translate it from my English into his Chinese. I then set off for downtown Kunming to shop.

The main intersection proves impassable. Across the street the Queen is still dining, the crowds are frozen on the sidewalks, and the army patrols the intersection, blockading the crosswalks. There's no way to proceed. I sink into a crouch. Another hour passes before the black limousines bounce out of the Villa gates. Everyone lunges forward on tiptoe. The prompter hangs from the first car like a sailor hiking out on a catamaran, urging the crowd to clap, and the Queen passes by me a second time, her hand stretched through a half-open window tentatively, like a limp flyswatter.

I cross the street and resume my march downtown, ignoring the wide-angle "Welcome" spelled out in flowers. The Welcome is not for me. I'm nobody again, a Big Nose without a limousine. Since there is no use attempting to visit any tourist sites today—they're closed for the Queen—I head for the department store, then return to the Kunming Hotel. Restless, I hire a taxi for the afternoon.

My driver speaks a wild version of English. He likes violent American movies, particularly one I haven't seen about a paraplegic with a missile-launcher built into his wheelchair. The title translated from Chinese is *Mr. No-Legger.*

We plot how we should circumnavigate the sphere of the Queen's influence. We soon end up on an unpaved back road, stalled for an hour among Neanderthal trucks, buses, and animal carts in what I believe is Kunming's first traffic jam. This historic bottleneck, attributable to the presence of the Queen in southern China, is not documented by the press. Most of what she must take credit for is involuntary anyway.

It is October 17, and the Queen of England has been marshalled through Kunming right on schedule. At 10:40 A.M., she arrived at Sanquingge Temple, halfway up the Western Hills, the entry point to Dragon's Gate, a stairway carved by hand in a sheer cliff above Lake Dianchi. She did not climb to roost in Dragon's Gate, however. Instead, at 11:10 A.M., she departed for Huatingsi, Temple of the Flower Pavilion, which contains statues of the 500 arhats, followers of the Buddha. While this is not the best set of 500 arhats in Kunming, the Queen was on a tight schedule, and under the lights and lenses, she could have done worse. At 11:35 A.M., the Royal Party retired for lunch at the Xiyuan Guest House on the lake. After a short xiuxi (siesta), she boarded a freshly painted pleasure launch at 1:30 P.M. and crossed Lake Dianchi. The press, filling a companion ferry, was served box lunches. The journalists were allotted boat tickets based on nationality: fifty to British and Commonwealth reporters, thirty to mainland Chinese, fifteen to the Hong Kong media, and fifteen more to "Third Country Journalists," including Americans.

It is now 2:30 P.M. and Her Majesty has just disembarked in Daguan Park on the northeast edge of Dianchi Lake. I'm still stuck in traffic. The Western Hills, which possess the shape of a reclining Buddha or a sleeping beauty, depending on one's fancy, rise on the west shore of the lake; Kunming begins on the east shore at Daguan Park. This is a fetching park, but the Queen can stay just twenty minutes. She and her husband Prince Philip are to plant rosebushes here of a variety called Volunteer in a ceremony to commemorate the Voluntary Service Overseas organization. Of a thousand VSO volunteers working in forty countries, twenty-two are teaching in China; of those twenty-two, four are teaching in Kunming and will be present at the rose planting, which I wish they would get on with so this traffic could start moving.

The Queen is due at the Institute for Nationalities at 3:10 P.M. This university was designed for the education and study of the ethnic groups in the province; most of its 20,000 students are non-Han Chinese. Seven hundred years after Marco Polo met with the "mixed population" of Kunming, Queen Elizabeth II will spend her hour among the Yi, the San, and the Hui. Then at 4:30 P.M., she will return to the Villa. At 7:00 P.M. she will attend the official banquet in her honor. At 8:45 P.M. she will receive an official presentation from the Governor of Yunnan. Tomorrow the Queen, Prince Philip, the Royal Party, various secret agents, the British military, and hordes of the official press will be bundled up, applauded, and flown east to Guangzhou.

Two of her seven nights in China the Queen has spent in the remote and obscure city of Kunming. I cannot imagine why. What did she see? Nothing of the life in the streets, certainly—its winding brick lanes, its pony carts, its work-ers' cafes, its traveling quilters on the sidewalk stringing an intricate loom. Nothing of the night markets, candlelit, stocked with flowers, tropical fruits, pork bellies, shish kabob, and sizzling hot pots. No corrugated metal sheds, open and displaying the latest T-shirts, sweaters, and blue jeans by day, closed and guarded at night by skinny cats tethered by cords. No open-air tailor shops where seamstresses invite you to sit down as they turn out severe pants suits and blazers on brand new treadle machines. Not even the best tourist sights. No time for the Stone Forest. No chance to hike to Dragon Gate, a vertiginous climb under the best of conditions; unthinkable with a hundred reporters and photographers nipping behind. The Queen of England did not come to Kunming to see either its most famous or its most telling sites; instead, she came to Kunming to plant a rose in the park.

— : : —

When the Queen left Kunming history was restored to its vacuum, and I was free to enjoy the sites she missed. I began with the 500 arhats, not at Sanquingge Temple, but on Jade Hill, at the Bamboo Temple (Qiongzhusi) northwest of Kunming, where Li Guanxiu, a sculptor, molded clay over wooden skeletons to compose the most demented congregation in China, perhaps in the world. Had Goya and Dali collaborated as sculptors, the 500 arhats of the Bamboo Temple would have been their masterpiece. The figures perch tier upon tier in two halls. Their faces twist and erupt into a vivid spectrum of exaggerated emotions from despair to joy to madness. Devotees ride oceanic crests on the backs of animals from nature and myth. Eyebrows two-feet-long sprout from perplexed foreheads. An arm streaks ten feet across the room, its finger shattering the ceiling of clouds like a lightning bolt.

My second stop was Daguan Park. I asked many people where I might find the Queen's rosebush. No one knew. No one cared. It was the day after.

My last stop was on the other side of Lake Dianchi, on the open face of the Western Hills. The way up to Dragon's Gate was crowded. The Chinese jostled up the stairs with their usual fearlessness, sweeping me from perch to perch, cave to cave, gate to gate. I reached the summit after several hours. Returning later by taxi, I kept seeing Kunming over the rim of the Western Hills as the road switched back. Once, as we came to a stop behind a bus behind a donkey cart, I had a long clear view of the city and I realized it looked like any city at this distance. At this distance, Kunming was as familiar a sight as the city where I was born, far away, long ago. All the differences disappeared and China disappeared, too. Then everything moved forward again, throwing me back with a jolt.

— : : —

My last afternoon in Kunming — my second Sunday — I spend at a teahouse run by minorities. The staff keeps an eye on me. They have persuaded an entire family to surrender the best table, the one overlooking the courtyard; when I protested, they seated me forcibly, their good deed done for the day. The first hour or so I am witness to a mystery: a young man is stationing and restationing three beautiful young models in Western dresses at changing points on a triangle in the midst of a crowd. As soon as he has one woman frozen in position just so, he rushes on to the next; but meanwhile the first one becomes bored, she breaks her pose, she rubs the blisters on her heel, she finally walks off. Round and round the triangle the handler goes, point to point. I have no idea what he is doing.

A couple finally sits down at my table. They want to practice their English. They are students at the National Institute for Minorities. They treat me to an ice-cream sandwich. When the Queen came to their campus, they say, she said something to both of them, but they could not understand what she said. It is her English accent, I explain. We all shrug.

The Chinese are strolling through the courtyard in their Sunday finery. They have no way to measure how fast, how very fast, their world is changing. They have not been away two years, in another world, so they lack my perspective. The only way you can see change is to not be there. Here, the high heels, the digital watches, the ice-cream sandwiches tell me it is another China we are now in.

Passing the "Welcome" garden for the last time, I stop to sample its scent. There's none. This is an odorless garden; the blossoms, I now see, are paper, silk, and plastic. Workmen are hauling the big balloons back to earth; they resist, like bloated kites that ate too much of the sky.

Was there a Royal Visit here? I see no trace. Even the Queen herself was in little evidence; I saw but a bit of her hand; it might have been a false limb. That would explain why the limousine window was rolled only part way down: to keep the limb from tumbling out while rounding a corner.

Poor soul. There she was, behind green tinted glass, veiled by lace doilies, sunken from view in the soft cushions of the back seat, clinging for dear life to the end of a plastic limb ripped from some hapless mannequin.

I am glad to have seen the passage of Official History from the cheaper seats, in the streets with the throng. Unshackled by the narrow lanes and calm seas of ceremony, I was rocked and thrown and dislodged and jarred, slowed and battered. Above all I felt buoyant, I felt free. I was part of another history, the big one, the one we don't see coming or going, the one offstage.

EAST OF MECCA

To reach Xi'an, I board an old prop plane in Kunming. An old woman offers me a banana. I refuse once, then accept. She has an entire plastic bag of bananas. She gives me three. I eat one and place the others in my pack. I notice that most of the passengers flying north have brought bananas on board.

I also can't help but notice the massive white refrigerator with the slightly curved dome which is strapped in where a row of seats has been extracted directly across the aisle from me. Bouncing in the turbulence, I am menaced by that appliance and the image it projects of a bizarre and ignoble fate—my fate: to be crushed to death by a loose refrigerator at 20,000 feet over China.

— : : —

Professor Zhong and an associate meet me at the Xi'an Airport. We pile into the same car, travel the same route,

skirt the same gray city wall. City of dust, thy servant returns. I should have learned from Marco Polo: he never went
back. I'm only staying two days, afraid that otherwise I'll be
here forever. Our car pulls boldly through the gate of the
Binguan. I'm ushered to a deluxe room on an upper floor. I
was never inside a hotel room while I lived in Xi'an. It's
rather stunning—a million miles from where I was then, a
room with a view.

Professor Zhong and associate are seated in my room.
They are both dressed in Western business suits, ties perfectly knotted. We have tea. They leave the shades closed. No
interest in scenery or travel. I withdraw the two bananas and
hand them over. They don't even bother to refuse. They peel
them and savor the insides, bite by bite. Bite by bite they sit
before me in their suits swallowing bananas under closed
curtains. They're gone in five euphoric seconds. I should have
brought more. I've forgotten how deprived the north is.

The rooftop disco is closed. No one else I know is in Xi'an
now. Rick Wacker is teaching tennis in Atlanta. Fred and
Rita have settled down in a small town near the shores of
Walden Pond; they have no plans to travel again. The Mac-
Larens are academics in London. Even the Africans have
graduated. Beyond the Binguan gate, the sidewalk is lined
with new hard-sell souvenir stores. There are taxis everywhere. It's even possible to find some Western food at Chinese stores. I'm alone.

I have one day to revisit a site in Xi'an: the terra-cotta
warriors, a temple, a shrine, a church, a cathedral, a
restaurant—whatever I chose. Just one. I very well may never
return.

— : : —

The Great Mosque seems too perfect to exist in Xi'an, as though a fragment of the T'ang capital was arrested here at the moment of its creation and sealed forever from the ruins and revisions of the centuries.

Fred showed me the way to the Mosque on my first day inside these city walls, and I used to return to it as often as possible: walk north off Xi Dajie, pass under the triple-tiered Drum Tower, raised here in 1340 by Ming rulers to sound the beat at the end of the day; turn again onto the narrow walled road which winds like the rim of a new moon. There the Moslem children always follow me, begging for coins and laughing; there, at a high weathered gate in the wall, they stop. They never follow me in; the crowds, the noise, the pace of the streets, the shops, the stalls all recede from the threshold.

Standing between the first two long courtyards of the Great Mosque, I see a worker sawing planks from an immense log. He is working slowly and deliberately, stopping sometimes to stare midway into the blank sky. He is completing restoration of a large wooden gate, an archway in the T'ang style, intricately carved, but he has erected it in a place where no entrance remains. There is only a wall on the other side of the new gate. Perhaps this gate commemorates an abandoned door.

I walk into the second courtyard the same way as in the past, through a stone archway where there are carved steles in the Song and Ming styles. I can look straight through the central arches of the third and fourth courtyards as through the sight of a gun now; I can survey the frets of towers and minarets and focus on the wide prayer hall at the far end.

It's like looking into the bottom of a well. Here Xi'an feels like its former self, like Changan, the old capital at the end of the Silk Road. The Vermilion Palaces are gone forever; the emperors are dust in their tombs strung across the northern plains of loess for a hundred miles, but the Great Mosque has endured. Nothing else is so exquisite: no temple, no church, no shrine, no tomb; not even the vaults of terra-cotta warriors and steeds are so graceful, so quiet.

Among the many who traveled the Silk Road from the West to this end of the world, the Moslems alone set down unshakable roots. Even the twentieth century with its republics, revolutions, and Red Guards could not uproot them. They proved to be the strongest because they came into China with no mission, they only wanted to live their lives, and so in time they became Chinese. They've been here since 651 A.D., the same year that Othman oversaw the compilation of the *Koran,* barely twenty years after the death of Mohammed. A century later, in 741 A.D., they built this Mosque—the supreme outpost of Islam in China.

The Moslems never dispatched any missionaries; they kept to themselves; they married Chinese women. By the end of the T'ang dynasty, they ceased to resemble Arabs. They became known as the Hui. Today the Hui still live in their own communities, wear white turbans, practice circumcision, and reject usury, divination, theater, and pork. They maintain their own schools, slaughterhouses, cemeteries, and mosques. Their neighborhoods are the oldest, their streets the narrowest in Xi'an. Every block has a communal

well—a handpump on the sidewalk. Their houses are low
and conjoined, with dirt floors and gray-tiled roofs. Their
streets are odoriferous and lazy. Vendors set up coal-heated
pots in the street and sell lamb on skewers, fried breads, fresh
yogurt. Without such cookery, Xi'an cuisine would be even
more ordinary, nothing but cabbage and noodles, dense
steamed bread and rice and the fat of the pig.

Underneath, there's bad blood, it's true: repeated re-
bellions, repeated repressions. A century ago, the Hui war-
lords seized all of northwest China and for eleven years ruled
Xi'an. It's hard to believe now, but their final defeat in 1873,
at the hands of the Manchus, was said to be merciless. Ninety
years later the Red Guards closed the mosques. The Great
Mosque has survived. The courtyards cover an area the
shape and size of three football fields, divided now as in the
beginning into four segments west to east. There has never
been a factory here, a school, a machinery lathe, an apartment, or a steamroller. The steles have not been defaced nor
the fountains hammered into splinters. Time itself has reduced this or that feature to ruin, but restorations have been
faithful to the source.

In the third courtyard is a triple-tiered minaret, the Tower
of Introspection (Shengxin). Early minarets were square,
unadorned buildings with jutting balconies from which
the muezzin called the faithful to prayer, but the single
minaret of the Great Mosque at Xi'an is eight-sided in
the style of most small Chinese pagodas and towers. Its
balconies are drawn in tight beneath blue roofs jutting
sharply upward. The arcaded porticoes, the brick pathway
linking the courtyards, and the arching gates and flanking

prayer terraces are all of stone and wood, intertwined like tattooed serpents.

The final courtyard is lined with austere pavilions containing many curious treasures—a gift shop catering to rich foreign visitors which are few; empty sitting rooms with finely-turned black laquered furniture; a restroom with the most astonishing toilet in Xi'an—a raised model with a carved wooden seat cover and a high domed back. It's a Byzantine throne.

One of the pavilions houses the present Imam. He oversees this mosque, settles disputes within its congregation, and is the chief butcher. He also appoints mullahs to teach from the *Koran*. Several mullahs are women. Moslem women cannot pray in the Mosque, but neither do they take the veil here. The worshippers in Xi'an accept the five pillars of the faith, practicing charity, observing the fast of Ramadan, and professing Allah to be the one true God. But perhaps none of the Hui have reached Mecca and only the Imam and the mullahs recite all their daily prayers at the Mosque. After more than a thousand years in China, the Hui have not created a new sect or bred a major prophet of Islam. Fridays, I used to see dozens of Hui men move from station to station toward the prayer hall, bathed and barefooted, their heads covered in thin white turbans, prostrating themselves before Allah, facing Mecca in prayer.

In a room near the Imam's residence there is a map of the world, a black cube at its center. China, displaced, lies beyond the western frontier.

The prayer hall is fashioned of wooden planks and rounded wooden columns, its entrance a wall of continuous doorways sealed from the outside by curtains of bamboo. The sweeping roof is paved in blue-glazed tiles. The central fountain resembles a bell-shaped dagoba, a type of tomb for saints. The walkway to the prayer hall is of white brick, inlaid with a base relief of fantastical designs. Two pools, now dry, mark the final approach; the path is a bridge, giving the illusion of a prayer hall encircled by a moat—a Chinese conceit.

I untie my shoes, setting them to one side, and step over the raised threshold. Within the prayer hall is the interior of the interior—another world, always in darkness. One knows this is a vast chamber even before one's eyes adjust: a ceiling as high and wide as the night sky; a sky adorned with carved coffers, with tapestries painted blood-red and blue.

My eyes always adjust quickly to the darkness here. The walls and columns are coffered and draped. Every surface is stamped in an intricate design, modules of the faith, the name of Allah in Arabic at every center. I can see a prayer niche, the mihrab, elaborately carved and facing Mecca. The floor is patched with myriad prayer rugs.

The door of the mimbar is closed, as always, and covered in a tapestry. My bare feet glide between rugs like blades on polished ice. This time I want to touch the walls; I have never seen any this rich, richer than gold or silver, warmer than an emerald, but I am an intruder. A man I did not see face down at the altar suddenly lifts himself into prayer. Barely breathing, I turn and walk out. His voice is lost in the chambered sky like a whisper.

The sunlight strikes the white stones and is crushed in dark creases. The courtyards recede behind me like screens in a painting, without depth or perspective. Every surface pulls my eye into its vortex of intertwining bands, flowing Arabic script, inescapable arabesques.

At the entrance to the Great Mosque, the sawyer is singing a song from a folk opera, his head tilted back to the blue sky. I step through the wall into Xi'an, a stranger.

EMPIRE OF
THE MOON

After revisiting Xi'an, I head east for Shanghai, arriving via overnight train at the fourth largest city on earth. Here, many say the next millenium is set to begin, but as an entryway to the future, Shanghai's North Station is not grand. It is not even hospitable. A disheveled complex of long platforms and chambers empties like a drainpipe into a crater shoulder-deep in idlers, touts, and weary travelers attempting to hail a handful of snarled taxis. After twenty minutes, with the assistance of a retired gentleman in a red armband, I manage to locate a ride. It requires another ten minutes for my taxi to nose its way into the street.

Once freed from the final queue, I'm bold enough to refuse my driver's proposal: namely, that I exchange a large amount of my hard currency for his local Chinese money. There are scores of black market moneychangers stalking the sidewalks outside foreigners' hotels throughout China, ready to exchange rolls of renminbi for FEC at rates of up to two-to-one; only in Shanghai, however, do I find so many cab drivers engaged in the practice. The cabs have become black markets on wheels.

I hold my ground: no currency exchange. The driver circles the train station, steers onto a back ramp, and dumps me out right where I started. We trade insults in two languages. I require another half hour to locate a cab not operating as a mobile moneychanger, paying four times the official fare — in FEC of course — to be taken to the venerable Park Hotel, a mile away.

When it was built in 1934, the Park Hotel was the city's tallest structure, its tea dances the rage, its chefs the best in Asia. Chairman Mao, on his visits to Shanghai, always stayed at the Park. Since it is now a month past tourist season, I have every reason to believe that there will be an empty room for me, but the front-desk clerk insists that only their most expensive suite remains. It is far too expensive, outrageous in fact, but, as the clerk cheerfully points out, rooms aren't easy to locate this late at night. As he expounds on the virtues of the one remaining room — "Tonight you will sleep in a suite" — I study the progress of a youthful cockroach scuttling across the marble counter between his outstretched hands.

I spend the next hour in the hotel's overpriced bar. When I return to the lobby, I'm told the same "suite story" by a second clerk. Up to this point, Shanghai has disappointed me: it's worse at accommodating foreign travelers than any other city in China; its taxi service is a disgrace; its big hotel is a model of high-handed disservice; and I'm about to be turned out into the streets.

I'm as much shocked as pleased, therefore, when a third clerk picks up the telephone and books me a room in a lesser hotel—the first time I have ever seen such a generous arrangement made between Chinese hotels.

This lesser hotel proves to be lesser in many ways, but it provides excellent service—perhaps because operations are in the hands of a younger generation. Their elementary courtesy enables me to ignore the general condition of my room. The hotel has three names: known locally as the Huai Hai and officially as the Qing Nian Hui (Youth Association Hotel), its stationery retains one of its older names—the YMCA of Shanghai. The YMCA dates from the same period as the Park Hotel and was originally built by French colonialists, who sandwiched it between the old French Police Station and the notorious Great World amusement center.

From my ninth floor window, I can see over tiled roofs into the courtyard of the Great World, where an opera troupe is concluding its performance. The Great World still attracts amusement seekers, but its complexion is now entirely Chinese, its offerings decidedly tame. Renamed the Shanghai Youth Palace, it boasts nothing more shocking than Ping-Pong, billiards, video games, ice cream bars, and ballroom dancing for singles. In the thirties, however, the Great World's attractions were more bizarre, at least according to film director Josef von Sternberg, who reported seeing gaming tables, slot machines, and shooting galleries with live ammunition on one floor; Taoist shrines operating beside opium dens on another; and midwives and prostitutes selling their services on a third. The featured exhibit in one auditorium was a whole stuffed whale; in another, there was an open row of Western-style toilets, arranged like a video arcade, with attendants on duty to instruct incredulous patrons on the proper way to sit and flush.

The YMCA now has its own novelties, too, though of a more mundane nature. On the wall above my bed, for example, a large insect is crushed like a specimen. There is also an ominous gap in the ceiling panels where the heat ducts could very well serve as a nightly runway for rats. My private bathroom has been recently remodeled, however, and I'm pleased to find the shower water hot and copious, even if the new toilet, tub, and sink are a resplendent institutional green, and the Western-style fixtures of Asian manufacture, brand name TOTO, tell me how far, how very far I am from Kansas.

The din in the streets never quite dies out; just before dawn, it rises to its full level—an unceasing clatter of voices, horns, brakes, wheels, shoes, and saliva smacking the pavement. I tumble into the marsh of sleep and wake in the twenty-first century.

— : : —

Old China has all but disappeared. A few dynastic monuments survive to bolster the tourist trade, but the great cities, shorn of their antique walls, are dominated today by faceless blocks of a massive modernization. Since the death of Chairman Mao, China's break with its past has accelerated; a new economic order, resembling that of the capitalistic West, has been implemented by a pragmatic leadership. Yet the future of the People's Republic of China—and with it, undoubtedly, the future of East Asia—is by no means certain. Wanting a sense of where China was bound as the decade of the 1980s neared its close, I decide to stay for an extended period in Shanghai, the commercial center of this new China and long the nation's most progressive metropolis.

My first impression is that Shanghai cannot possibly become the capital of the next century. It is not magnificent; it is not even strikingly modern; most emphatically, it is neither efficient nor beautiful. From the harbor, Shanghai rolls back like a low, flat housing project ten miles square, simmering in the "Yellow Dragon" of its own industrial exhausts. Cloaked in gray, it looks deathly ill. On the other hand, I cannot deny that the future of the planet might well congeal in this thick, colorless caldron. The ingredients of the next century are all here—the sprawling factories, a bit of high tech, rampant pollution, a vast, cramped population—and these are now being stirred by the brash, arrogant commercial spirit which has set the Shanghainese apart from other Chinese for decades. Even Shanghai's visible past is unique in China, and comports with its drive toward a Westernized future.

Shanghai's skyline and many of its streets are European— the architectural legacy of foreigners who colonized, partitioned, and ruled the city up until World War II. Little of China's own cultural heritage is on view in Shanghai, but much of its contact with the West is embodied in granite and stone, imparting to the city the suggestion of international decadence for which it was once celebrated.

Recently, moviegoers in the West have been treated to a stunning recreation of this old Shanghai in Steven Spielberg's *Empire of the Sun*. The sweep and scale of this "Paris of the Orient" were made for the wide-screen. When I first walk

Shanghai's avenues, I immediately feel at home, as though the movie has been a documentary of current events. Very little theatrical makeup had to be applied to peel back fifty years of socialist reconstruction, and the crowd scenes might have required no staging at all. The ordinary chaos of the streets is like an unconscious rehearsal for headlong mass evacuation; the fifteen thousand Shanghai extras who reenacted the panic in the streets (on the day after Pearl Harbor, when the Japanese took the city) probably had little trouble looking convincing before the cameras.

In the autobiographical novel by J. G. Ballard, upon which Spielberg based his film, the author recalls how old Shanghai looked and felt to a privileged child of British diplomats on the evening of its final dissolution. Ballard dubbed Shanghai the "electric and lurid city more exciting than any other in the world." The streets were "lined with nightclubs and gambling dens, crowded with bar girls and gangsters and rich beggars with their bodyguards." The center of the city was a phantasmagoria of international spectacle:

> Hundreds of Eurasian bar girls in ankle-length fur coats sat in the lines of rickshaws outside the Park Hotel, whistling through their teeth at the residents who emerged from the revolving doors, while their pimps argued with the middle-aged Czech and Polish couples in neat, patched suits trying to sell the last of their jewelry.

Ballard also recalls how his parents took him to the Cathay Theater, the world's largest movie house, for the premiere of

The Hunchback of Notre Dame, where "there had been two hundred hunchbacks, recruited by the management of the theater from every back alley in Shanghai. As always, the spectacle outside the theater far exceeded anything shown on its screen," and Ballard remembers he "had been eager to get back to the sidewalks of the city. . . ." The sidewalks still attract; on the pavement is where one senses the sheer force of the future unfolding from its shameful and vital past. I have never walked in streets so congested. Space itself seems to contract into crowded cells; everyone is linked shoulder to shoulder; we collide at random like molecules in a chamber of dense smoke. This surge has no obvious meaning; it seems to have no end. It is single-minded and unstoppable. Here, indeed, might be where the next century begins, at least for China.

In the past, China has absorbed intruders, wrapped them in its borders, and eventually assimilated them completely, but China must now turn itself inside out. To strip the West of the wealth and technology it needs, it must become more like that outside world than ever before in its history. By virtue of its progressive character, Shanghai is China's leading edge in this mission, its sharpest point of contact between East and West. It is here that one looks for rainbows to bridge the various worlds and dreams; here, too, where one often looks in vain. The glitter of international modernism which now decks the avenues of Hong Kong, Tokyo, Singapore, and Seoul has not yet returned to the streets of Shanghai.

Nanjing Road is the Fifth Avenue of Shanghai, the main shopping street of the nation. A million shoppers walk here daily, half of them said to be out-of-town Chinese. The main attractions are silk shops and department stores residing behind a commercial facade which dates from the days of the International Settlement, its foreign appearance muted by decades of neglect.

It takes me an hour to walk a mile east toward the harbor, an hour of determined forward motion; my shoulders ache from sheer contact with other shoulders, which serve as grinding stones in this assembly line of shoppers. I find temporary refuge in China's largest emporium, the Number One Department Store, which consists of four floors of poorly displayed, utilitarian sundries and wide central stairways, each with a spittoon or two strategically placed on the landings. For out-of-town Chinese, this store is legendary; goods made in Shanghai have long been imbued with the highest reputation for quality. Most items I see are inferior by international standards, although their variety has increased remarkably over the last few years. Perhaps the most notable new offering is Western-style cosmetics. Many young women of Shanghai now use skin conditioners, moisturizers, lipsticks, and eye makeup. Styles have a Western flair—the Shanghainese are still China's fashion plates—and women frequently wear earrings (not long ago a sign of bourgeois decadence). The most daring are attired in bright sweaters, high heels and black tights. Leg-warmers and running shoes are popular, too. Even hairstyling has gone Western: every salon provides blow-dry cuts and permanents. The young who still sport blue workers' jackets and lack boutique trims stand out as provincials. If salaries were higher, Shanghai would be overrun with its own yuppies. As it is, professionals make less than $100 a month; they can not afford BMWs; very few, in fact, have their own telephones. Shanghai is a seething bay of ambitions, of first-world consumers locked in a third-world economy.

I reach the eastern end of Nanjing Road at noon. It is still presided over by a landmark of the thirties, the green-towered Peace Hotel, a masterpiece of art deco. Until Liberation in 1949, it was known as the Cathay Hotel, the swankiest hotel in the Far East. Wide, revolving glass doors front its lobby; the uniformed staff is gloved in white; many of the rooms retain their original plushness. The first-floor bar once again features jazz from the era of swing, with one or two players who performed in the thirties on hand. The only modern note is struck just outside, where the Peace Hotel is ringed by the ultimate expression of big-city free enterprise: a chorus of black-market moneychangers, young men clutching vinyl valises. As each foreigner is catapulted from the revolving doors, they attack like hyenas, as often as a dozen times in half a block. The moneychangers who know a little English have devised elaborate strategems. Under the guise of "practicing English" (a national obsession), some will accompany tourists for blocks at a time, pointing out good restaurants and shops in the area, and then, as an afterthought, plead for an exchange of currency. I was seldom far from the tentacles of these unregulated money seekers. They reminded me of writer Pan Ling's observation about the essence of old Shanghai: "Its idol was mammon and its heart lay wholly in the marketplace." The moneychangers have taken this dictum to heart. They now occupy the posts deserted by the high-class streetwalkers of the thirties, the loquacious sing-song girls.

The chief vehicle of Shanghai's burgeoning economy, however, is not its street trade, but its long harbor — the Huangpu River runs northwest to the Wusong Estuary where the Yangzi River flushes it into the South China Sea. A third or more of China's trade passes through the seventeen miles of wharves, shipyards, and cranes of the Huangpu. Maritime traffic is as dense as the foot traffic on Nanjing Road; it is also more international.

In the afternoon I book a three-and-a-half hour cruise on the Huangpu at a wharf directly across from the Peace Hotel. The Pujiang Touring Service ("developed to complete an abundant service system of amusement above the water") proclaims in its brochures that views from its cruise ship "are so attractive that you will be fascinated to stay there," but that is shamefaced hyperbole. The Huangpu is one of the world's great rivers, one of the busiest as well, but also among the most foully polluted. Nine thousand factories feed it and four million tons of untreated sewage are discharged here annually. The cruise company cites an ancient poem which likens the waves of the Huangpu to a thousand flowers, but in the eyes of a modern passenger the river raises "griminess" to a new level, just as Nanjing Road takes the term "crowded" to its logical extreme. River and ship are mired in sludge and greased in gray particulates.

A first-class ticket entitles tourists to a quiet, enclosed lounge on the upper deck and access to the open rail outside. There I pull up a wicker chair, drink tea, nibble on fruit, nuts, and chocolate bars, and watch the endless procession of tankers from Iran and Iraq, and nearly every nation: of motorized wooden junks, long chains of unpainted barges snaking up the middle of the channel, bearing raw cargo under their lines of laundry. I'm cautioned not to snap pictures of the Chinese gunboats, missile-launchers, and mysterious military relics, such as a pre-World War II submarine in dock, gray and bulbous as a whale. The unloading facilities and dry docks are not immense nor entirely modern, but they are as endless as the silk shops and steamed dumpling restaurants I strolled past earlier.

After two hours, my ferry reaches the new harbor complex at the river's mouth. The buildings are already ghostly pale, and the hands on the harbor clock tower frozen in place. In the estuary beyond, I see hundreds of ships at anchor in a sea of vapors, as though they are waiting for time itself to begin.

"Where the sky and water connect closely," the cruise brochure assures me, "not only the situation is grand but also the scenery is picturesque. These all make you satisfactory to your trip." Those most "satisfactory to their trip," however, are undoubtedly those Chinese passengers in first class who never leave the lounge, hardly glance out on the traffic of the river or at the smokestacks beyond, who watch closed-circuit TV from the sofas, consume the snacks, and fall asleep in their own private sea of tranquility. Here, beyond the tide of the future, they find a refuge. When the Bund returns to view, its buildings rising from the mud-white flats like the husks of a desiccated civilization, they stand up reluctantly and disembark like sleepwalkers.

The general grayness of Shanghai is compounded on the Huangpu; the river seems to choke on its own commerce. This is not a stream of beauty, nor does it show the slightest promise of becoming so; but the future is not necessarily a thing of beauty, not even something one would love or desire. Individual passion belongs to the past, I think, or perhaps to the shadowy margin between river and Bund.

The Bund is a term which the British borrowed from India to describe the muddy embankment of a river; as applied to Shanghai, it refers to the European skyline along the Huangpu River, the domes and towers of Shanghai's old Wall Street, which still houses banks, bureaus, and custom houses. Facing this monolithic skyline, on the embankment itself, is a pedestrian walkway. Those who are not bankers or cadres in the new regime come here with their sweethearts hand-in-hand, arm-in-arm, even cheek-to-cheek, and embrace in the bowers of plane trees. By dawn, the lovers of Shanghai have disappeared into the shapeless suburbs. The embankment is taken over by crowds retracing the venerable forms of taiji. For a moment they shadowbox in a private dance which requires no daring partner, no vision of the West. On the Bund, however, the very old and the very new are as discreet and delicate as dusk and dawn. In the center is all the tonnage of the working day.

— : : —

The next morning, tired of walking the streets of Shanghai, I decide to take a bus across town from the harbor. Consulting a map in Chinese, I locate the correct bus stop and number for my destination, then join the unqueued cluster at the curb. When the bus pulls up and its doors unfold, there is a single-minded surge; those getting on meet head on with those getting off. Somehow I squeeze on, and standing, announce my destination (a cross street) to the roving con-

ductor. She receives my fare and hands me a paper ticket.
After ten minutes on a Shanghai bus, even the streets seem
spacious. There are never enough buses, and the streamlined,
fully robotic subway promised for the early 1990s will accommodate just a third of Shanghai's commuters, hardly
enough to make a serious dent.

I am heading into the heart of the Old French Concession.
My destination is the Jinjiang Hotel, a graceful complex
dating from 1931. Recent guests have included Nehru, Tito,
Thatcher, and the last four American Presidents. Nixon
signed the Shanghai Communique there in 1972, opening the
door to China. On a more humble scale, I stayed there in
1984; I remember that the bathroom was lined in black
marble.

The Jinjiang complex is highly Westernized. Its shopping
arcade features an upscale restaurant (Café de Rêve) and
boutique (A Belle de Chine), as well as the nation's finest
minisupermarket, the Jessica, where I now find such rare and
precious commodities as Chiclets, Pampers, and—stacked
beside the Marlboros at the check-out counter—imported
condoms, three-to-a-pack. The original lobby is rather dark,
but the coffee shop is bright enough: an exact and shiny
reproduction of those you would find in any Holiday Inn
today, except for the slow service.

I decide to reserve a room in the old north wing of the
Jinjiang in order to spend my last night in Shanghai—exactly
a week from now—in decadent surroundings. A uniformed
desk clerk helps me. I review the rate schedule, select the
cheapest room, and begin to fill in the reservation form,
printed in Chinese characters. The desk clerk is impatient

with my need for assistance. He picks up the phone and shouts into the receiver. I ask if he understands my request — the cheapest room for one night, a week hence. "Of course," he snaps. "Now pay in advance." I place FEC on the counter. "You have a reservation," he says. "If cheaper rooms are filled when you come back, we will give you a more expensive one. OK?"

This is not OK. The more expensive rooms are two and three times the price I have advanced. "I want to reserve a room at this price," I insist. "Can't you do this?"

The clerk glances down at the computer screen. His face explodes. He yanks the reservation form from my hands, tears it in half, and slams it down on the counter. Then, perfectly composed, he stands nonchalantly before me until I walk away.

Luckily, I have somewhere else to go. The Jinjiang is surrounded by remnants of the French occupation — shops, villas, and apartments with creamy white walls and tiled roofs, glazed in orange and red. A block north is the Lyceum Theater, rebuilt in 1931, the most venerable of Shanghai's hundred cinemas, and across the street is the Jinjiang Club, once the Cercle Sportif Français. I find the club closed, however, and partly demolished; a new club is scheduled to rise from its ashes. Too bad. The original was the most refined relic of Shanghai, replete with art deco interiors, a lavish Japanese restaurant only the rich could afford, and an indoor Olympic-sized swimming pool. Chrome and plastic will quickly supplant stone and granite.

The Jinjiang Hotel itself is undergoing thorough renovation, too. Next door, in a vast vacant lot, I survey its newest

acquisition, the round Jinjiang Tower Hotel, forty-two stories above street level. A few blocks east, a similar tower
nears completion—the Shanghai Hilton. New towers
crisscross this city, yet there are hundreds of foreign mansions still standing in Shanghai, whole neighborhoods of
them, especially in the French Concession. They have been
converted into schools, offices, barracks, and factories, but
many are still splendid on the outside and resemble those
used as sets in Spielberg's *Empire of the Sun*. In certain cases,
even the lavish interiors have survived more or less as rich
foreigners and diplomats left them a half-century ago during
the Japanese occupation. Still, they do not figure in the future
of Shanghai; like the Jinjiang Club they await demolition.

One mansion listed in the guidebooks as the Shanghai Arts
and Handicrafts Research Institute is now frequently visited
by tour groups, but its premises are difficult to find on one's
own. I must stop at a dozen unmarked gates and inquire at
each guard post for its whereabouts. I'm directed up one lane
and down another. Eventually I stumble onto it. The
gatekeepers point me down a driveway to a long, narrow
sidebuilding, which proves to be the factory outlet.

The crafts produced under the umbrella of this Institute are
displayed in deep, dusty, unlit glass cases along an outside
wall. A number of clerks, eating lunch, ignore me. When I
finally inquire after a restroom, I'm told there's none. (The
phrase for "don't have" in Chinese is *mei you*, often invoked
when the clerk doesn't want to be bothered by having to fulfill
a request.) I wander outside and try the door to a three-story
building, so massive that at first I don't realize it once served as
a single-family residence. The door opens into an antecham-

ber staffed by several artists. One is painting bamboo shoots and songbirds on T-shirts. I find the bathroom—a tiled lavatory with a pedestal sink and a Western-style toilet.

It's strictly by chance that I've entered the main building of the Shanghai Arts and Handicrafts Research Institute. Now I'm cordially invited to explore the entire mansion at my leisure. A curving staircase leads upstairs to a spacious central room, stripped of furniture except for a few display cases and a large table with chairs. To one side is a hallway of closed doors—once the bedrooms or studies or sitting rooms of a wealthy foreign family. I open a series of these doors at random; inside each I discover a group of artisans at their crafts: wood carving, paper cutouts, dough art figurines. Each work room is unrestored, unheated, and each has the empty feel of temporary occupation.

Directly off the central chamber, through French doors, is what was once a lavish dining room. The chandeliers no longer function and the embossed wallpaper is just beginning to peel at its seams, but the room retains its grandeur. The white enameled woodwork is unchipped. Over an enormous fireplace no longer in use, I'm confronted by a portrait of Ronald and Nancy Reagan in needlepoint, framed like an oil painting. The dining room has in fact been given over to this craft, with worktables and baskets of yarn draped helter-skelter across the parquet floors.

The back of the mansion contains a spacious marble veranda with stone stairs down to an acre of lawn, a garden, a pond and artificial stream. There are artisans stationed on these grounds, too, fashioning the skeletons of life-sized ceramic cranes.

The temperature is barely above freezing today. I think of the mansion Nien Cheng owned in Shanghai up until the nightmare of 1966, as described in her best-selling memoir of political persecution, *Life and Death in Shanghai*. Cheng and her daughter lived in a three-story, four-bathroom house. They owned a private telephone, embroidered linen table mats, rosewood furniture, and a small collection of fine antiques. Such spacious living and luxury are unimaginable now, even in an era which encourages free enterprise and the accumulation of personal wealth. The mansions of Shanghai have become shared and crowded property—a fitting and necessary thing in a city that literally cannot build apartments at a pace equal to its population growth.

Chilled, I take to the streets. Although I'm not lost, an old man stops me. He gives me directions to Nanjing Road. Attired in coat and tie, he speaks superb English. His voice is deep, highly cultured. The instant I thank him, he disappears, like the apparition of a vindicated Galileo.

— : : —

When you are a true outsider, more happens by chance than by design.

In the evening I set out for one of Shanghai's most famous restaurants, but I fail to locate it in the dark labyrinth of pedestrian overpasses. I turn quickly back toward the YMCA on Ziyang street. A small, brightly lit restaurant catches my eye. I enter at once. It must be new. The walls and tables are unstained, the paint unpeeled, the atmosphere festive. It is frequented by young people, many of them well-dressed couples. I'm the oldest customer, the only foreigner.

Several young women wait on me. They are pleased that I can read the English on their bilingual menu. All that's missing are the prices. It turns out that a Coke costs as much as a main course. Coke is now all the rage; a few years ago, not many Chinese drank Western soda.

Seated in the center of the room like a prize, I'm under scrutiny from every quarter, but I'm left entirely alone. In fact, I'm doing most of the staring: a young couple have brought their own bottle of Chinese champagne. It takes them ten minutes of brute force and repeated assaults to remove the cork. We exchange smiles.

When I pay my bill, stand, and walk to the door, the entire staff lines up to bid me farewell, in precise and pleasant English. One waitress puts her whole heart and soul into the only English phrase she has mastered, "Welcome to our restaurant," while another, through a slight mistranslation, bids me farewell with: "Thank you for coming to our hotel." The couple with the champagne give me what has become the "in" sign among the young in China—an upward thrust of the thumb.

By contrast, the next night I end up dining in the more established splendor of the south wing of the Peace Hotel. The restaurant is called the Crane Longevity Hall, an oddly evocative name, almost as strange as the name of another place I ate, in Canton—Mr. Beef Seafood Restaurant, with its three life-size bronze cows grazing out front. The Crane Longevity Hall is remarkably well-preserved, its turn of the century elegance still palpable. Nevertheless, Shanghai is eager to find the shortest course to full modernization, and it is not sentimental about what stands in its way. This old wing of the Peace Hotel is already condemned; a forty-story glass and steel tower, the first real defacing of the Bund by the architecture of the future, will take its place.

The senior waitresses of the Peace Hotel are always nattily attired in white blouses and slit black skirts, their nylon stockings lumpy with the presence of winter long underwear. Seated on a landing curtained in lace, I can look down discretely on dozens of diners. I watch the table occupied by a Chinese couple in their late thirties. There's no doubt from the way they dress and the manner in which they dine that they are "overseas Chinese" probably from Hong Kong. When their drinks arrive already opened—a can of cola, a bottle of beer—they refuse them. They wipe off the dishes with their own tissues. The wife pours a dab of beer on each plate and rinses it; the husband withdraws clean forks and spoons from his pocket. The restaurant chopsticks remain untouched. When they do not like the appearance of an entree, they send it back. Perhaps what China refuses to borrow from the West it will someday adapt at the behest of its own returning compatriots—notions of hygiene and service, for starters.

As for the gimmickry of a technological future, however, the Shanghainese require no prompting from "overseas Chinese." They flock to the latest electronic scales, for instance, which are supplanting the mechanical weight machines in many of the older stores and hotels. The itinerant gentlemen who carried even older contraptions from street corner to street corner are obsolete. The electronic devices dispense with spoken and printed fortunes; they flash your weight in LED readouts for all to see, with the confidence of a digital

H. G. Wells. The most eager customers approach the machine with such faith in its chips that they bother neither to remove their coats nor to set aside their shopping bags. With the same faith and verve, Shanghai steps onto the scales of its own future, even if the readout is no more accurate than the measure given by a fortune-teller in an alleyway.

— : : —

The weight of opinion in Shanghai is that China will overtake Japan in the next century. By then, China will rival Russia and America as a great world power. It is not the opinion of Dr. Fu, my next door neighbor in Xi'an, who was finally released to join his wife after threatening to kill himself in protest. We meet again in the least modern section of downtown Shanghai, in the Nanshi (Old Town) district which, during the years of foreign occupation, remained untouched.

Old Town is now a popular tourist stop precisely because of its antiquated appearance. Located in the heart of a city which is otherwise dominated by the colorless concrete highrises of China's reconstruction and the run-down museum pieces of its Western days, Old Town was once enclosed in a three-mile wall and moat constructed to protect the Chinese from Japanese pirates in the sixteenth century. The wall was toppled in 1912, however, and the moat filled in with a circular boulevard.

Still, when one passes beyond the modern parking lots filled with air-conditioned tour buses, most traces of modernization disappear. A bazaar of street vendors, meat and vegetable markets, craft stores, and dumpling restaurants engulf and engorge the Temple of the Town Gods. The Nine-Turn Bridge and the Wu Xing Ting Teahouse, which the guidebooks erroneously herald as the picture-perfect model of the blue-willow plate pattern, are emblems of Old China. Next door is Yu Yuan, an intricate, highly polished, almost garish Chinese garden of pavilions, rockeries, and an undulating dragon wall in the classical style. It is more crowded than Nanjing Road, and always closed for lunch, like China itself.

Dr. Fu has reserved a table for us on the third floor of the famous Lao Fandian (Old Restaurant) near the Nine-Turn Bridge. The windows are too dirty to allow us to take in the view, however, and the interior has all the charm of a bus station. Dr. Fu tells me that his son has just graduated from a four-year program in International Business in Beijing, but he's been assigned to teach English at a college in the provinces rather than to pursue his vital specialty. As for Dr. Fu, he too is in waiting; he has not yet obtained permission to study abroad. He lacks sufficient political capital in Shanghai, much as he did in Xi'an. While he believes that China will never democratize itself, he is pleased with the general policies of the leadership. "We will not go back to the days of Mao," he proclaims. We discuss the difficulties of unemployment, overcrowding, and inflation which has hit Shanghai particularly hard during recent economic expansion. Nothing much is being done to solve the housing crunch. The problem it seems is the corruption of freewheeling Party bureaucrats. Dr. Fu, his mind on his son, especially laments the absence of choices; still, his pessimism is tempered now; he thinks that China can improve.

Two young men at the next table, watching us closely, whisper excitedly. They are dressed in new suits and ties, their hair styled in curls. They goad each other until one speaks to me in English. He asks the usual questions about my job, age, number of children, how often I had been to China, my hometown, and then, nearly giggling, tells me that he and his friend have been accepted as students at Brigham Young University next fall. There's only one hitch. In order to buy books, they'll need foreign currency — will they not? So would I be so good as to contribute — "Change the money?"

Dr. Fu bolts to his feet. He barks; the two "students" bark back. A few fried eels are still warm on our plates, but we stride out of the Old Restaurant without a backward glance. Outside he says, "I hate this place." At first, I think he means the restaurant, or maybe the moneychangers, but he means he dislikes Old Town. There's no charm in dirt streets and communal privies for him.

We take a bus across town to the new Sheraton Hua Ting Hotel: twenty-nine stories of glass in the shape of an enormous S. Dozens of Mercedes, Jaguars, and Santanas (a sedate sedan produced at a Volkswagen plant in Shanghai) wait outside. Inside are 1018 of the city's best rooms, culminating in a thousand-dollar-a-day Presidential Suite.

When Dr. Fu enters the shining lobby, his voice drops to a whisper. This might be as close to the future, or to the West, as he will ever come, and he glows in the moment. Gardens, teahouses, temples of the town gods are but quaint attractions which the next generation will enclose in its streamlined malls. Today Dr. Fu is swimming the length of the

S-shaped lake of his dreams, completing the new symbol of Shanghai.

— : : —

I depart the next day on the S.S. Shanghai, one of China's three best "luxury" cruise ships. All were purchased secondhand from the West; all now serve the sixty-hour Shanghai-Hong Kong route. Belgian-built in 1957 as the S.A. Cockerill-Ougree, the S.S. Shanghai has changed little since its P & O days; it seems to enjoy middle age in the Mare Orientale beyond the Bund. The crew is earnest; the dining room, bar, theater, and lounges serviceable.

My stateroom is worn but spotless. The private bath is original, down to its bidet. The sole annoyance is a weak-flushing water closet which the steward can not revitalize. Later, I test all the toilets in the common bathroom on the deck below; they, too, can not quite clear themselves, constricted by the residue of neglect.

The swimming pool on the upper deck looks in off-season like the excavated foundation for a small house, empty save for two broken wicker chairs and a Coke can rattling at the bottom. The grand piano in the ship's first-class lounge also bespeaks the force of time unopposed by regular human maintenance: its keyboard has been looted of ivory, each yellow key neatly cropped of its top layer of silky skin. I plunk a slightly out of tune key. Suddenly the sheer scale of Shanghai's geography, population, and resources overwhelms me; when it recedes, I see the sour vision of one possible future—a gray vanishing point where Los Angeles merges with Shanghai in a marginal sea of low skyscrapers and dust.

Out on deck, I fold up my map, but even in departure I cannot escape the immensity of Shanghai. My ship requires half the night to reach the estuary, crammed with a thousand ships like anchored stars. It takes another four hours to cross into the South China Sea. Then, just before dawn, I wake; in the porthole I make out a monstrous vessel, approaching us dead on. I stand and watch, helpless as not so much as a single sign is exchanged from either side. At the last moment we slide by each other like Earth and Moon.

THE BLOOD
OF GHOSTS

The next time I return to China it is the spring after the massacre in Tiananmen Square. As April lurches forward toward May, an ill omen—a dust storm from the north, bloated with desert loess as fine as pulverized locusts—covers the city like a tent and closes the airport. Described as the worst such cloud to envelop Beijing in half a century, it arrives in the late afternoon, about the time I board a plane in Shanghai, two hours to the south. I am anxious to reach Beijing today, to see how it fared the hard winter of austerity and martial law; anxious also to meet up with a colleague from my days in Xi'an—Ivan MacLaren, now a diplomat. Instead, I must spend another night in Shanghai.

Even the next day, I am delayed. Although the dust clears enough for Beijing to reopen its airport, Shanghai now finds itself at the mercy of nature. Repacked in the same motionless plane, it's announced that the Shanghai runway is "broken"—one end of the strip dug up by a construction brigade. We can take off in only one direction, but to do so we must wait for the wind to change course. We wait three hours for the wind to change; it finally whisks us away. When we land, the dust in China's capital is still suspended between Earth and sky, but it has thinned so that all the usual traffic—cars and trucks, buses, bicycles, and horse-drawn carts—can circulate in the aftermath. Many bike riders and pedestrians have wrapped bluish netting completely over their heads and even their hats, tying it at the neck. Beijing resembles a city of beekeepers.

I have forgotten how dismal a modern capital Beijing really is, flat and sagging, like a deflated dirigible laid over a table without edges upon which are concrete blocks of houses, offices, and institutions. These unpainted legacies of China's brush with Russia's monumental Stalinist architecture—China's first postliberation model—have been updated but not improved, and they exhibit no Chinese characteristics, save a lack of maintenance. Beijing possesses no skyline, only these low buildings and broad boulevards which retrace the concentric grid of old palaces and moats, the walls and gates that enclose the Forbidden City, and Tiananmen Square in the center of the Central Kingdom.

It is a grim setting, an impoverishment of the senses. Yet there is no lack of movement among its denizens. At street level I feel the familiar dynamism propelling the ceaseless crowds, the same energy I felt throughout the progressive 1980s. There are torrents of buying and selling, of bus brakes and arguments and even of laughter, in a city of shadows, of gray cement, of foul air. There is no beauty to speak of, but there is life in Beijing.

It is a life of caution, to be sure. The political and military lightning which struck down the democracy demonstrators in the darkness of June 3rd and 4th at the close of the decade stilled most citizens. Few talk to me. Americans are a rare sight now, and those who ask about our sudden disappearance do so in a wounded, uncomprehending manner. Beijing's grand new hotels stand ready; they stand empty. The euphoria which rippled through China's tourism industry before the catastrophe in June has left its towering marks east of Tiananmen Square as far as the diplomatic quarter: the splendid husks of new hotels, with water you can actually drink from the tap. But who will drink? It will be years before Americans return, if they ever do.

After watching the fate of democracy and freedom in China on television, Americans have lost their fascination with the Great Wall, and what is now inside that enclosure disappoints them; it turns their stomachs. The West is much more interested in seeing where the Berlin Wall crumbled than where the Great Wall still stands. One American leading a press group around Beijing tells me that when she finally explained the American feeling to an interpreter, the young, shining-faced girl burst into sobs.

— : : —

There was a single episode during the black winter after Tiananmen Square worth noting: the cabbage crisis. Plainest and lowliest harvest of the field, cabbage has sustained millions in northern China over the centuries. It is still what pilot bread once was to the common sailor: the only dependable sustenance during a long monotonous voyage. Thus, since 1949, the government has subsidized the production of cabbage as an expression of goodwill to its people. The citizens, in turn, have responded by snapping up the winter's shipment at two cents a head, dutifully storing the bounty in every cellar and cranny — until this past winter, that is, when, as the staple rolled into town on galleons of green and gray trucks, the citizenry cast a cold eye upon it, letting cabbages pile up unpurchased on street corners, like so many bowling balls.

It was a spontaneous boycott, a sharp retort. The leadership's only answer to worsening economic conditions seemed to be an echo of Marie Antoinette in the East: "Let them eat cabbage." There was certainly enough of the stuff. Central planning, suddenly back in vogue with the triumph of the hard-liners, induced farmers to reap a bumper crop, and in November the capital was swamped with some 400,000 tons of cabbage, heaped like cannon fodder. As Beijingers stepped around the latest unwelcome arrival, soldiers from the People's Liberation Army, conscripted to stack the surplus heads, had plenty of time to check each other's weight on the empty produce scales.

The mayor, Chen Xitong, ordered every citizen to purchase 660 pounds of cabbage immediately (an astonishing figure, even in China, where the per capita consumption of cabbage each year is normally a mere 66 pounds), but the patriotic vegetable was by now so loathsome that even the local bureaucrats refused to buy their mandated quota.

The most popular suggestion for disposing of unpurchased cabbage was to stockpile it in the new athletic facilities being completed in and around Beijing, part of a construction frenzy intended not only to make China look good when it hosts the Asian Games but also to bolster China's bid for the Olympic Games in the year 2000. Most Beijingers believe that their city is out of the running for the Olympics, of course, that the money spent on lavish sports facilities should be reallocated to alleviate the housing shortage, and that new stadiums are useless, except for stockpiling cabbage.

In the end, after weeks of foot-dragging, consumers did buy plenty of the vegetable because they feared that with the economy sinking as swiftly as the temperature, the fresh alternatives from the south could no longer be counted on—they might become snarled in the red tape of a brave new decade and left to rot. The cabbage crisis ended peacefully, but a spirit of protest or at least of resentment, seemed to be reborn.

— : : —

Few signs of outrage, however, have survived the spring thaw. I see none in Beijing; I've seen only a few in other cities. One taxi driver I sat behind in Shanghai had the boldness to play a celebrated Hong-Kong pop protest song about Tiananmen Square, but he never turned around to eye me, and he probably thought he was safe, that I wouldn't recognize the song or understand what it said. Earlier, while pausing on a street in Canton, I was overtaken by a young man with a boom box who cast me a look, raised his fist, and shouted in English the word "freedom," but he walked on quickly, not looking back; he didn't expect nor wait for a response.

In Beijing, the clamps are tighter still, at least on the students, whom I never see downtown. They've been told to stick to their campuses, miles out in the suburbs. Some Chinese hotel workers explained to me that the students want to believe that their demonstrations inspired the revolutions in Eastern Europe. Even if these students are right, such a fond hope is their sole consolation now — a distant, immaterial legacy.

I find that the winter cabbage has been replaced by clots of radishes ripped fresh from the earth and dumped on street corners, and that the people are resigned to eating their allotments, along with the less visible fruits of their bitterness. Perhaps they are biding their time, waiting for the next shift in the mandate of heaven, waiting for the old leaders to die. Like their ancestors in other dynasties, Beijingers accept but do not like their position. They resent the spectacle they have become, out of step with the rest of the world, with Eastern Europe, with Russia, even with Albania — a submissive audience to the Peng & Deng show. The iron curtain is torn down, but, as a popular Chinese song puts it, the Great Wall will never fall.

In China politics and people's lives run on separate but parallel tracks, as they have for thousands of years; the Chinese make this useful, if painful, distinction instinctively. Americans do not. Americans keep everything on a single track, cleaving to their political machinery. If they are led like train cars by their engine, at least they feel they can demand a say in where they stop and where they are bound; in fact, they can remove the engineer if they wish. The rider in Beijing knows better. He knows that until the two tracks cross again it is better not to look up or ahead, that it is best to be patient, even if the locomotive starts running backwards or endlessly circles the roundhouse of Central Planning.

I make my own circuit of Beijing hotels, some Chinese-managed, others glitzy joint ventures with a few dozen expatriates on hand, mostly from Singapore or Hong Kong, with two-year hardship contracts. A new Japanese joint-venture hotel on Changan Avenue proves to be as spotless as I imagined; it is from one of its upper floor windows that someone emptied a clip on a straight line into rooms everyone knew the Western journalists lived in. At the Jianguo Hotel, farther down Changan, I happen into the lobby on Sunday and find it stuffed with foreign diplomats and executive branch managers enjoying a perfectly ordinary brunch recital: a middle-aged Chinese soprano belts out popular as well as light classical showstoppers. In the massive Beijing Hotel nearest the square, the magazine stalls are replete with propagandistic pamphlets entitled "Report on Checking the Turmoil and Quelling the Counterrevolutionary Rebellion"—official terminology for the June Massacre. I also spend a fair length of time just standing in the lobby of The Palace Hotel, staring at the arched white marble bridge and waterfall. This is Beijing's most dazzling hotel, as dazzling as anything in the Orient; it is also one of China's more unlikely joint ventures, a marriage between the prestigious Peninsula Group of Hong Kong and the People's Liberation Army, which might, looking down the road, become an Old Soldiers Home with bidets.

— : : —

I telephone Ivan at the embassy, and he picks me up in his car, which he drives himself, a feat many long-term expatriates choose to perform—somehow avoiding mayhem and suicide at intersections where great gates of bikes seem to open and close without warning or reason. It's like driving on the sidewalks in Manhattan. We eat dinner early in a local vegetarian restaurant, where one orders at a window and washes it all down with local beer from a liter bottle. It's similar to restaurants we frequented in Xi'an. Ivan asks if I want to walk on Tiananmen Square.

I do. Ivan drives the car up a street alongside the Great Hall of the People. There is very little traffic in the area, but he constantly looks over his shoulder and complains we are being followed. He parks. "I know I'm paranoid," he explains, "But can you blame me?" He mutters a clever commonplace, to the effect that just because you're paranoid doesn't mean they're not out to get you.

Glancing north across Changan Avenue, I can see Chairman Mao's colossal portrait on the gate to the Forbidden City. Under his stare, on the far edge of the square, the flag of China is being lowered in apparent consonance with the setting sun. A throng has gathered, not to protest but to entertain themselves by watching the lowering of a flag—a barometer of the state of nightlife in the capital.

There is no Goddess of Democracy left to face Mao this year, of course, and I can no longer remember, despite still and moving pictures, exactly where she stood. It is no wonder I cannot place her, because the square is now as disorienting in its emptiness as it was in its fullness. A few people stroll across its expanse. The paving blocks are all exposed, an endless patchwork. We walk up the stairs of the Monument to the People's Martyrs where the students maintained their command post, where the first wreaths and scrolls appeared on another day in April, where a single young protestor in a suit was arrested this year.

From the slight elevation of the monument, the view unnerves me. Tiananmen Square is a haunted expanse. It is haunted by the living as well as the dead, although for me these ghosts have been ghost-images from the start. Because the world's media focused fifty days on the selfsame square, Tiananmen is more than familiar; it has become its own televised double. Being here merges the image with its reality. I am stepping into the frame where the months of occupation, of daring, of triumph, of hope, of foreboding and disaster occurred. The emptiness of that reality frightens me. Tiananmen Square is so immense when unoccupied that I am incapable of imagining it filled; but of course it was once filled—by its own city of students and workers.

Ivan saw it for himself. He begins to lead me around the main platform of the monument. He expounds: how alive and charged it felt under the light poles at three in the morning as he was conducted deep into Tiananmen Square through streets marked in the minds of those living there, a burrow through humanity into a square sacred to the politics of China. The students went further than anyone before them; they seized the square whole and made it a human mass. Soldiers of the King took it back in a matter of hours under darkness; platoons from the provinces shod in sneakers who seldom aimed their bullets; formations of armored carriers and tanks come to chase, come to scorch, come to scoop. Certain paving blocks in the Square bear black patches, as if recently charred.

The flames even reached up the stairway of the monument. Chunks of stair tread are missing; there are ragged lines where the edges were snapped off. One can imagine the size and thickness of the missing pieces and strips, but not the monster that broke them off. Ivan keeps pointing to the broken treads, the missing pieces, the black marks, saying "See this? And this?" but never explaining, not even suggesting what happened. What happened, even if known, is inexpressible.

Dusk deepens. The young People's Liberation Army guard assigned to the monument asks us politely to go down. The monument stairs are roped off every evening in frail twine.

The loudspeaker poles in Tiananmen Square are mounted with video cameras now. We can see, as we are supposed to see, the figures of the security force coming forward atop the Great Hall of the People, black silhouettes. This is the backhanded pressure of an occupation, of martial law imposed by China over its own capital, now lifted and replaced by hair-trigger intimidation. It is clear that nothing will happen — that no demonstrations will be initiated or develop this summer, perhaps for many summers. The anniversary of last year's martyrdom will pass in silence. The students are defeated.

But "lies written in ink can never disguise facts written in blood," Lu Xun has warned. Another uprising is on its way. This is as certain as the empty square, as the voices under the stones.

It could take a decade; it could take a century. A century is nothing. In Xi'an centuries barely count. It's as if China possesses far more than its share of time, and when required can withdraw any length of time from its vaults. Then, with perfect indifference, China can ride its celestial tracks almost forever, toward a point without parallax.

On the other hand, everything can go to smash in an hour, in a day. A storm of dust can arrive without warning off the desert, grounding everything.

The Chinese have settled in for the long haul. Westerners are getting out. The MacLarens are evacuating. Ivan's car is on the auction block. Their next post is Moscow.

The China decade is over. Those not tied by death to the past are moving away, even those only moving in circles. Suddenly I feel I was never here at all. Looking for the way back in, I hear a bell in its tower at dawn and a drum at dusk. There's a bolt of lightning in the distance, the glint of a self buried on a plain as flat as glass. I see a city the shape of a tomb where nothing dies, layered in lucent dust, and a moat paved with black stars. The old capital is nearly colorless, gray and drab; yet its individual features are vivid, and each facet has an extraordinary depth. In America, where the primary dimension is space, one is naturally drawn outward; in China, one is always drawn in and the eye itself is altered — but, after all, I have journeyed from the old capital to the new. In the center of this new China a fire is burning which cannot reach us, a dream is dreamt in which we do not yet appear. Everything spins away from me in circles, like time, like China, unable to hold the future, haunting a square of the past.